Star: The Story of One Duck's Rise to Fame

Sue Hayman

Star: The Story of One Duck's Rise to Fame

An MKSP eBook/May 2014

Published by Master Koda Select Publishing, LLC
www.masterkodaselectpublishing.com

Cover design © Amy Winfield
Cover photographs © Julia Masters Photography -
www.juliamastersphotography.com

ISBN-10: 0985983884

Acknowledgements

A big thank you goes to Amy Winfield. She approached Barrie whilst he was out with Star and asked if she could write an illustrated children's book featuring Star. Having readily agreed, I then conversed with her and the plan was for me to provide her with details of some of the events that had taken place for her to base her book on. Little did any of us know that once I started writing I couldn't stop! A story had begun and just kept going. Throughout the time of writing and since, Amy has been a real supporter, and we are looking forward to seeing Star's illustrated children's books coming out soon.

Thank you to Emma Perry and all the team at Little Bridge House.

A massive thank you to Star and Barrie's supporters and friends – you have truly made a difference to Barrie's crusade.

Thank you to my publisher – Master Koda Select Publishing, for not only having faith in me in the first place, but all the support they have given throughout the whole process.

Thank you to Barrie. I do not court controversy easily. On most things I manage to be the greatest influence in our lives, but with all that has happened Barrie has been the driving force, to keep going, keep moving forward. If it had been up to me, I would have run a mile when some of the troubles first started, but not Barrie. Even with his health suffering, he still hasn't given in. I have the utmost respect and admiration for what he has achieved and what he does.

The last thank you has to be for Star. Without doubt he has kept Barrie going, brought him back to joy in life again, and thus has enhanced both our lives enormously. He is a very special gift presented to Barrie and I feel blessed to have been part of it.

This book is dedicated to all of Star's supporters and friends.

Chapter One

Where we lived, although rented, was almost our dream home – let's say a nine out of ten on the wish list. The house was old, dating back to the eighteenth century, and still had some real character features despite being gutted and refurbished several years before. It was situated in a lovely rural hamlet and best of all, had some land. Not loads of land and for most people it would have been classed as a large garden. Not in Barrie's eyes. This was enough territory to have animals on, especially with the couple of old outbuildings and a greenhouse that was half falling down. To Barrie, it just screamed of having some kind of smallholding. Within a week of moving in, we already had four layer hens. That was something we had talked about for years and years and now we had them. We could now have our own free range eggs. Barrie also really wanted some Indian Runner Ducks. They were like normal ducks, except that they stood upright. Originally bred in India, the clue being in the title I guess, they worked the rice fields. Farmers wanted the ducks to eat all the nasty insects that ate the rice plants, but didn't want them to fly away to someone else's field, so they bred them to be incapable of flight. Because of this, the ducks evolved with longer necks, longer and sturdier legs, and could move at considerable speed to try to outrun any predator, hence the name *runner* duck. We first found out about this breed from a local tourist attraction and Barrie was on a mission to track a breeder down. After several unsuccessful weeks of trying, he eventually found someone that had bred them, but didn't have any at the moment. However, what they did have were some goslings.

I have to confess I wasn't too keen on getting geese. I had heard stories from people who had them in the past or knew of people that had kept them and apparently they could be quite unfriendly and even aggressive. Although they were seen as a good protector for a home, I really wanted animals that were like our three dogs – cuddly. Only nice animals in the Hayman household please.

Anyway, overruled, I went along to the farm to see the goslings. Despite my reservations, I am afraid I was as smitten as Barrie. There were twelve of them, with four adult geese as protectors. It was an amazing sight! They had a huge field to roam around in, but we were confident that they would be happy in our much smaller plot. We agreed to come back the following day to collect four of them.

The next day very excitedly, we properly met the goslings, who were now separated from the adults, housed in a stable. Yes, next to some horses - quite surreal! We could hear the geese in the distance somewhere and could tell they were unimpressed that their little babies had been taken away. Now time to choose which four to have...

Well actually, Barrie had already decided. We were to have all twelve. Nightmare! I had never owned geese in my life let alone having twelve baby ones to look after!

Due to their size, we managed to fit them into two crates and got them home. They were so cute. And thankfully our three dogs – Meggie and her two Border Collie sons, Drake and Genghis – all liked them, too. In actual fact, the two Collies felt it was their duty to keep them rounded up altogether. They would not let the goslings out of their sight and guarded them with their life. Thankfully too, the four hens (or "the ladies" as they were now known – well truth be told we had actually gone so far as to name them Mummy Sylvia, Mummy Phyllis, Auntie Miriam and Lady Mabel – much to the amusement of our mums) didn't mind them being around either. With the small outbuildings, we had two little homes for our animals and Hayman's Farm was developing nicely. In fact, to me Hayman's Farm was now complete. However, that all changed a few months later...

Chapter Two

Barrie was driving down the lane when a car stopped in front of him. He could see some commotion ahead. Getting out to investigate, he saw a duck with ten ducklings standing in the middle of the road.

The guy who had stopped in front of Barrie explained that he had seen this same duck and babies a few miles up the road several hours earlier, and that he hoped ducks had nine lives just like cats as he was sure they must have been nearly used up by now. What to do? By this time, a number of cars from both directions had stopped. As it was the countryside, none of them were angry about being delayed. Most of them got out to discuss what to do next. Whilst they were trying to come up with a plan, the mummy duck decided that she had had enough and just flew away, leaving her ducklings to fend for themselves. The motorists now had no choice but to round up the ducklings and get them to safety. One of those who stopped was local to our hamlet and suggested that Barrie take them back to join the hens and geese. Barrie didn't need much persuading. As no one had a pet/animal carrier stashed in their boot, someone emptied out a box that held beer cans. Although it wasn't big, the ducklings themselves were about half the size of the average adult hand so they would all fit in nice and snug. A handful of people, including Barrie, then started trying to collect the ducklings. Despite their young age and the fact that they must have been knackered from all the endless walking they appeared to have done already that day, they were decidedly agile and managed to dodge each and every hand that came down to get them. They really didn't understand that they were being rescued and were not in danger. Exhausted and frustrated, Barrie and his trusted team were all starting to feel a little helpless. Time to bring out the big guns. Barrie opened the boot and got Drake out.

Drake was born from great Collie blood. His grandfather was a national award winning sheep dog and his father was a well respected local sheep dog. Meggie, his mother, was more Australian Kelpie than Collie and therefore more ditzy and had no desire or talent for sheep herding. Thankfully, Drake recognised this in his blood and had already proved from a very young age that he was a good sheep dog.

Obviously though, these were not sheep. They were ducklings, and tiny ones at that. Barrie knew he was taking a risk and also knew that he was potentially up for much ridicule. He could see out of the corner of his eye that his trusted team thought he was a bit bonkers.

No one could come up with a better plan so Barrie looked at Drake and said, "Come by," meaning go around to the left – a term used by shepherds.

For Drake this was sheer bliss, and two of his favourite things – to work and to please his master. However, there was a problem. What was he meant to be doing and where? He couldn't see anything other than people, hot and bothered ones at that, and cars. Confused, he looked up to his master not knowing what to do. Barrie got down on his knees and pointed to the little ducklings.

"Oh, I see it now," Drake seemed to say. So very slowly and carefully, he started rounding up the ducklings one by one. It was still a little tricky as they were so small, but gradually all the ducklings were in the box. Well done Drake!

They didn't have too far to drive back home, which was a good thing as the ducklings were not impressed at being in a small box, and most of them had managed to get out and were running around on the seat and down into the foot well. By the time I got home from work, Barrie had found a cage and successfully had them all settled. They were funny looking things. Tiny balls of fluff, brown in colour, and nearly all of them had a big white cross on their back, making them look like a load of moving hot cross buns!

Only nine of the ten ducklings survived. One of them seemingly couldn't handle the trauma of leaving its mum and being hunted down to safety. The others grew into lovely little ducks. They were soon roaming around our land alongside the hens and the goslings, which were also growing up fast and were now a mixture of yellow fluff and bright white feathers. But we knew it wouldn't be long before they would need to move on to their own lives, to bring up their own families. We wondered how to do this. Should we take them down to the burrows and set them free? We had checked on the Internet and discovered that their breed lived near the sea. Their mum may have come a few miles inland just to hatch them safely and maybe lost her way and couldn't get back again; hence wandering the lanes with them.

The quandary was taken out of our hands when one day, a couple of the ducks simply just flew away. They didn't get very far on their first attempt as we had neighbours knocking on our door saying they had the ducks in their back garden. So again, Drake went in to help round them up and bring them back again. Eventually all of them left and this time, successfully. To this day we can only hope that they are parents of their own ducklings.

Chapter Three

Having the ducks for that short space of time only made Barrie more determined to have the Indian Runner Ducks. His wish came true as winter arrived. The local tourist attraction needed someone to look after their Runner Ducks over the winter when the attraction was closed. Barrie jumped at the chance. At the same time, we also found that we were now owners of a menagerie of chickens and a couple of cockerels. Each time I came home from work, I would see a few more new arrivals. It got to the point where I had absolutely no idea as to what I would find when I came home! Hayman's Farm was now close to bursting and something had to give.

The geese had been growing fast, and contrary to what I had heard, they were absolutely lovely. They all had different characters and we were very attached to them with some of them even having names.

However, they were getting just too big, and twelve were a little excessive after all. One morning with the decision made, Barrie and I were up very early and with the help of Drake, we rounded up eight of the twelve geese into the back of Barrie's truck. I went off to work with a tear in my eye as they went off to market. When they got there it was quite a sight, even to the farmers, as they watched a Collie shepherding these eight geese into the dedicated stalls and then guarding them while Barrie went off to do the paperwork.

When I got home from work, surprise, surprise, he hadn't come back empty handed. There were two adult Indian Runner Ducks and two ducklings. He was chuffed to bits that he had finally found some of his own.

That Christmas there seemed only one obvious present to get for Barrie – an incubator. I also bought him some stocking fillers of books about breeding ducks, chickens, and geese. Over the next few days we went about getting the other bits and pieces we needed to become breeders, including lamps, thermometers, etc. It was not long before the incubator was switched on with Indian Runner Duck eggs inside. It had begun. Having brought two puppy litters into the world a few years before with Meggie, we were now hoping to bring new life into the world again.

Through the books, we knew roughly how long it would take for them to hatch as long as we made sure the temperature was kept right and that they were turned regularly. Unfortunately, I had not been able to afford an all singing and dancing incubator, which meant we had to manually turn the eggs ourselves at regular intervals throughout the day. This was Barrie's job, who happily accepted the challenge.

Meanwhile, it was one of the worst winters the area had seen in decades, and we found that we were not so much snowed in, but iced in for a few weeks. My car had been stranded several miles away, having not been able to get up the hills, and Barrie's 4x4 didn't like the ice either. There was more than one occasion when we found ourselves sliding sideways down a hill – me with my eyes tightly shut and wishing desperately to be somewhere else, while Barrie sang Christmas carols, enjoying the ride. Goodness knows what the dogs were feeling in the back!

The geese, ducks, and chickens didn't like the weather much either as they couldn't get to the grass to feed as it was all iced over. You see, most of their food came from the grass. They were our lawnmowers to the point where we no longer owned one. Thankfully, we didn't lose any of the animals during that cold spell.

The time had come and we anxiously checked on the eggs far more regularly than we needed to. The first thing I would do on coming home would be to race upstairs to the spare room, the one that used to be my office but was now the new nursery, in anticipation.

And there it was. Looking through the little round glass window in the incubator, a small chip in the shell of one of the eggs. And then it moved! It was finally happening. Barrie and I, both with a glass of wine in our hand, got a couple of chairs and sat with bated breath, to see what a newly hatched Indian Runner duckling looked like. Much to our disappointment, it didn't happen that quickly. The one thing we hadn't taken note of was how long it takes a bird to hatch from an egg. Literally hours and hours! That said, it was still more exciting than anything on the TV.

To help them along, Barrie would spray a little water on to soften the shell to make it easier for them. Our hearts were going out to them. It seemed like such hard work to come into the world. They literally had to eat the inner shell for the outer shell to eventually crack.

Finally we saw something poke out of the shell. What was that? A leg? A beak? They were making noises too, as there were several now starting to appear, as if they were all talking to each other, egging each other on. Very difficult to explain the noises they were making. It sounded something like a muffled tweet.

After a very long wait, the first one finally hatched. The little duckling appeared, and to our surprise looked like a miniature dinosaur: something straight out of Jurassic Park, and very gangly. How had it once fit into the egg now that it had unravelled itself? At first it just lay there, probably completely exhausted from the exertion of getting out of the egg, but then it popped its head up, gingerly stood, and moved away from its egg. When to intervene? Could we go in and get it yet or should we wait? We had no idea what to do. We left it for a little while, but then went in and gingerly picked it up. It was still warm and wet, but we carefully placed it into its new home – a plastic container with a couple of soft towels in the bottom and a very powerful lamp shining down to keep it warm and to dry it out. This little gawky creature appeared content with the attention, and thankfully was happy for Barrie and I to take turns to have a cuddle, with the occasional snout of one of our dogs poking through, who were just as excited and curious as we were. We cuddled the little creature whilst watching through the glass at the development of the others. After about half an hour, the next one arrived. We put the first one back in its new home and delicately took the next one out. Where the first had been yellow in colour, this one was dark brown. Unsure what was best, we put the newborn in with his older sibling. Even though he was only minutes old himself, he seemed aware of the company and although he let him have a little space at first, he then went over to it and sat beside him to keep him warm. Over the next few hours more siblings started coming out, in varying colours – either yellow, brown, or both. Whether it was just purely down to beginners luck or design by nature, all ten of the eggs we had put down successfully hatched. By now it was the middle of the night, but neither Barrie nor I cared as it was a labour of love – just like with Meggie's puppies several years earlier who also, incidentally, decided to have her first litter of eight throughout the night.

As each one emerged, the same thing happened. The older ones would literally take the newer ones under their wing. They had become a little gang who totally looked after each other. As they dried out, the colours came out more and they looked a lot less Jurassic and more a gangly fluffy thing! All three of our dogs watched everything that had taken place, but the most surprising was our youngest dog, Genghis, who was Genghis by name and Genghis by nature – a cheeky chap – who took on the role of nanny and seemed to feel it was his duty to look after them. Not only had we brought ten new lives into the world, but had also now seen a completely different side to one of our dogs.

We put some chick feed and a shallow bowl of water down for them and said a prayer as we eventually went to bed.

Barrie, as a light sleeper, had been up to check on them several times in the night. He needn't have worried though, because when I got up the next morning the ducklings were all full of life and very noisy! They were happily playing, eating and drinking.

We had a cuddly puppy toy called Mini Drake that had already acted as nanny to the rescued ducklings several months earlier, and was now reinstated for these new ducklings. We hoped it would be some comfort to them. As time went on, it seemed to be more of a climbing frame for them and a spring board out of the enclosure!

We did get to have some cuddles with these little ducklings, but these were not for long as they were making it very clear that they didn't really like humans. Yes, they seemed to understand that we made sure their water and food bowl were topped up and their enclosure was kept clean, but other than that they were just very happy with their own company. We knew this had been the case with our adult Runner Ducks, but were surprised that this behaviour was adopted so early in their life.

As they got bigger so did the container, until they were eventually large enough to join their fellow ducks outside. However, some were sold. You see, Indian Runner Ducks are very easy to keep. Unlike other ducks, they don't need a big pond. We had a small pond that we built, but for the first few months we just had a couple of plastic containers filled with water and both the ducks and the geese were content with getting in the tubs to clean off. As long as you had grass and somewhere safe for them to sleep at night, they thrived. Having said that, if you ever get the chance to properly see ducks in the water – even in our little pond – you would truly understand the phrase "water off a duck's back". The first time we saw this, we were mesmerised. The ducks would dive under water and as they came to the surface, the water became almost like bubbles on their feathers as it slowly drained off.

As the months went on, more and more eggs were put down, including chicken and goose eggs. Unfortunately we were never successful in hatching the geese, but we did get a couple of chickens. It seems that chicks and ducklings rub along just fine. The only downside is that the chicks copied the ducklings and that meant going for a swim. We lost a couple of chicks where they had tried to swim in albeit the shallow tub of water, but as they were never born to swim and had the wrong type of feathers, they would drown. It was heart-breaking, but no matter how many times we tried to tell them, the chicks just wouldn't listen! There was one such chick that had nearly drowned several times. It was born at a time when we hadn't had so much success with the eggs and only one other hatched – a duckling. They became inseparable. Even with no others to follow, the duckling instinctively started swimming, so the chick did, too. Somehow though, it survived each time. We had a buyer interested in the duckling, but we had to explain to them that if they wanted the duckling, they would have to take the chick too as we believed they should go as a pair due to their obvious closeness, but also explained about his death wish with water. They happily accepted the challenge. A few months later we heard that as the chicken grew, he still loved the water. Several times they had had to resuscitate it, and eventually on the third time, it died. Some chicks just never learn.

Chapter Four

It was now coming into summer and was a lovely, warm sunny day. We were sitting in Hayman's Farm – our own little haven. All the animals were around us, including our three dogs, while we enjoyed a glass or two of wine. We started reminiscing and laughing about the time Barrie had been working on the stone wall outside the front of the cottage, and Drake was happily minding the geese – rounding them up more like! All twelve of them. It was a hot day and this was thirsty work, so Barrie had been drinking a beer whilst doing the build. He popped in to go to the toilet and closed the bathroom door behind him even though there was no one else at home. But then he heard the geese. How come? He knew they could be loud, but not that loud. What the hell was going on? As soon as he could he opened the door and there they were – all twelve geese in the kitchen and a very smug looking Drake.

Aren't I a clever dog! I have done my job and I have brought them to you, daddy!

"NO!"

Geese can poo for England, and here they all were, right at the bathroom door that was situated at the end of the kitchen. And they had pooed all over the kitchen floor.

Barrie then had to encourage Drake to shepherd them back out the front door. He was far from impressed and hadn't told me about it straight away. Only the day before, we had mopped and polished the floor so it was gleaming. As Barrie was clearing up the kitchen, he was just thankful we had a downstairs toilet as God only knows the carnage it could have brought if Drake had tried to shepherd them all upstairs, which we were under no doubt Drake would have done! So although it had been the wrong thing to do, in Drake's eyes he had done the right thing. Barrie found himself telling Drake,

"Thank you, Drake. Thank you very much!"

Anyway, right now all was very peaceful. Well, we found it peaceful as we found the noises made by the geese, chickens, and ducks going around their business of eating grass as very soothing. They were also fascinating to watch, similar to a soap opera through their interaction with each other, all rubbing along together. We were one big happy family. Although my job was stressful, Hayman's Farm was where I was able to unwind. Life was good...

Chapter Five

But it wasn't really. In fact, only for me, life was pretty good. I had the life work balance that I wanted. But for Barrie, although he had successfully bred and raised a menagerie of animals (to the point where I and others regularly referred to him as Dr Doolittle with his instincts and ability to relate to and rear animals with little or no previous knowledge or experience), he was still very frustrated. He was now officially a pensioner, having just turned 65, and he was not a happy bunny. He didn't want to get old. He didn't feel old, and definitely didn't look it, except for his body letting him down.

At that point, we had been together for thirteen years, having met in Australia. When I met him, he had already led a very extraordinary and action packed life. He had emigrated out there in his early twenties with his first wife and their baby daughter, Nicola. His life had taken a very different path to what could be classed as normal. He had done many skydives, and literally thousands of scuba dives – both professionally as a scuba instructor and personally, he worked with the Navy and the police and eventually on Stradbroke Island in Queensland. Barrie certainly had his share of excitement on and under the water, including several hairy encounters with sharks. It was while he was on the Island that he started working in the film industry as film crew. It was suggested he go in front of the camera and a new career emerged. He worked in films alongside Richard Chamberlain and Jackie Chan, and also played a doctor in a long running medical soap. On the back of this, he moved to Australia's capital for film-making – Melbourne. It was there that I met him. Having graduated, I had worked in London for a few years, but felt I was getting into a rut so I decided to pack my bags and travel instead.

We met whilst staying at the same backpackers hostel in Melbourne. I was 26; he was 52. Very quickly we realised we were destined to be together and within a few months we were back home in the UK.

We settled in Kent for a few years, remaining close enough to London for Barrie to go in for auditions. He picked up parts here and there for films, TV, and commercials, but unfortunately his career didn't take off as much as it should have. The TV world was quickly turning into Reality TV rather than just on real talent alone. Although you could accuse me of being biased, he was and still is, a truly gifted actor. It was this disappointment that encouraged us to move away from it all and hence, end up in Devon.

My job at the time had hit the ceiling of how far I could go and we were both desperate for a change. Although we were broke, we had booked a long weekend camping in Devon. It was only the second time in nearly four years that we had gone away and so we were both really ready for a break. However, Barrie had a bad feeling about it. The days leading up to our trip, he was totally obsessed with getting a car harness for our dog, Molly, which was really strange as she had travelled in the car for years without a harness. With the car packed up, and the dog in the harness, we set off in the early hours of Friday morning. It was a bank holiday weekend so we wanted to miss most of the traffic. We had been on the road a couple of hours, still very early so there was incredibly little traffic on the road. Literally we just got onto the A303 heading West and it happened. A stag ran out in front of us and we hit it head on. The poor creature went up onto the bonnet, the kicking legs missing the windscreen by millimetres, back down the bonnet and under the car. So what saved us? Two things. Firstly, the fact that Molly was in a harness, and therefore didn't fly forward into one of us or the windscreen, but secondly, the experience Barrie had from driving through the outback of Australia during his time as a sales representative, where he regularly had similar encounters with kangaroos. So apart from the stag and the car – both were completely written off, we were unharmed. Shaken, yes. Disappointed and gutted, yes. At our wits end, yes. A holiday for us? No. We were towed back to Kent and spent the weekend at a very low ebb. But on bank holiday Monday, Barrie announced,

"If we can't go on holiday to Devon, then let's go and live there instead."

I laughed, and light heartedly agreed, but the seed was sown. Within two months we had packed everything up and started our new life in Devon. Looking back, it is amazing to think what you can do if you are determined enough. We had no money, and no friends or jobs down there. We just took the plunge and hoped for the best.

Since then, the acting career had become pretty much non-existent as we were no longer near the hub of all the activity and Barrie got increasingly frustrated. He had been working as a presenter at a local tourist attraction, so had something of a stage there, but it was nothing like being in front of the camera and truly performing. I felt helpless. There was not a lot I could do to help.

Barrie had slowly been going into a depression over several years. In addition to that, he was seriously ill only a few years before with a long stay in hospital, ending with a triple heart bypass. This brought a limitation on getting any further regular employment. Having said that, he survived and also recovered very quickly, so he obviously knew that, deep down, there was something out there to live for.

Chapter Six

We had had the incubator, plus a couple more that we had bought or been given, for about six months now and had seen several lots of ducklings and chicks hatch. This brought us to a point where we were now pretty relaxed about the whole thing. We still loved the idea of new life and I still went and cuddled the ducklings when I got home from work. But we were a bit laid-back on timings now. We kind of forgot to put the dates up on the wall chart we had at the beginning, so we didn't really know when the next batch was due. Barrie would continue to turn the eggs, but for both of us now it was a surprise if and when one of them started to hatch. We also had experienced whole batches not hatching, and because we never quite understood what had gone wrong, we also didn't take it for granted that anything would hatch at all.

It was a very normal morning. I had woken early, washed and dressed, fed the dogs, had breakfast, let out and fed the animals, and then gone off to work. I hadn't been in the office long when Barrie called to say a new duckling had arrived. Great news! It had been a little while since the last batch. He said that it must have hatched in the night as it was bright eyed, alert and dry, and was looking up at him when he came over to the incubator. Although he can usually talk for England, Barrie doesn't like talking on the phone, but this morning he was sounding very animated. He said he needed to go as he wanted to get back to this little duckling.

When I got home, I had the usual waggy-tailed welcome from our three dogs, but Barrie was nowhere to be seen. I called out and heard Barrie say he was upstairs.

When I opened the door to the nursery, he was lying on the floor. Huddled up right in front of him was this little fluffy yellow duckling. It took me a while to realise that there were a couple of other ducklings that were also on the floor, but they were almost over the other side of the room huddled together. Barrie was so keen to show me some photos that he had taken earlier that day. When I looked, I couldn't believe my eyes. There was this little yellow duckling dancing! Well, that's what it looked like, and posing for the camera. Barrie was full of it, telling how this little one had literally started performing in front of his eyes almost as soon as he had been put on the floor. I asked about the other little ducklings that had hatched shortly after and he told me how, unlike before, this first duckling had not seemed interested in them, had not really paid much attention to them. As the others arrived, they instinctively huddled together, but not this one. He almost stayed aloof. I must admit I didn't really believe this and am ashamed to say that I wondered if this was in Barrie's imagination, despite the fact that the truth could be seen even now with the other ducklings away from both him and this little yellow fluff ball.

I couldn't deny that this little one had spirit. He stayed very close to Barrie all the time I was watching. Looking at the photos, I commented that this duckling appeared to be a little star.

"Star," he said. "That's a good name for him or her. Yes, Star by name and Star by nature." I couldn't disagree.

That evening I didn't see much of Barrie at all. He even insisted on having his supper while staying with Star.

Chapter Seven

As the days went by, Barrie spent a lot of time with Star. I could understand the attraction – here was another performer, just like him. Previously, he had wistfully talked about having one of the geese tame enough to be with him and maybe travel in the car with him to places. Wouldn't that be novel? But I was worried. Star was not spending much time with his siblings. Barrie tried to explain to me that he had watched them all together, and for some reason, his siblings didn't seem to accept Star, and Star didn't actually seem to be bothered by this. I was not totally convinced even if the evidence suggested otherwise.

They were now a few weeks old and it was a lovely warm day. As three of his siblings had new homes to go to, their owners came to collect them that morning. Star and his one remaining sibling were put outside in a small enclosure. I had insisted that Barrie put in one of the other older Runner Ducks to act as a mummy figure. We had unimaginatively called her Lame, because she was a bit of a hop along and had been for months, so never quite kept up with the others.

Barrie reluctantly did as I instructed and left Star with his sibling and Lame in this enclosure while he did some chores outside. However, every time he walked past the enclosure, even I noticed that Star seemed to only have eyes for Barrie and watched him wherever he went, and whenever Barrie continued on, Star made such a racket. But again, doing as he was told, he left Star there to keep the other duckling company while we popped out to do some shopping. A few hours later, we both went straight to the enclosure. There was Star waiting for him, but no sign of the other duckling. Lame was hiding in the undercover part. We looked everywhere until we noticed a small hole in the mesh and realised what must have happened. We had lost yet another little animal to the damned rats.

We had always been worried about a fox getting to our geese, chickens and ducks. That's why they were always put away at night, but we had actually found that it was the rats that we needed to be more worried about. Surprisingly, it had been rats that had been the killer of a couple of ducklings and chicks before and even some of the more vulnerable older ones.

That was it now. That was the sign if ever there was – the rats had come in and taken the one other sibling, but had left Star. I had to admit defeat and agree that Star was special. With no encouragement from me, Barrie found a medium sized cage and brought it into the kitchen. Star now had his own bedroom, and we were now without a kitchen table - which Barrie declared that he had never liked anyway, as he relegated it to the back garden!

Star was now part of the family.

Chapter Eight

Even with my doubts, I have to confess that there was obviously a massive bond between the two of them. They were inseparable. Wherever Barrie went, Star went too. He was still only a little duckling and couldn't walk too far, so Barrie got around that by putting him in his top pocket. Star happily stayed there with his head sticking out or would go down and have a little nap. He went with Barrie to the shops, to the beach, on the farm rounding up sheep with Drake, and even to the pub. Many people didn't notice Star was there. He even went into the local supermarket. Some of the check out staff noticed and were thrilled. Star wasn't seen as a health threat as he was only in Barrie's pocket after all. It was while he was in the supermarket one day that he noticed two women who were giggling and pointing. Barrie had forgotten that he had a duck in his pocket and wondered what that was all about, but ignored it nevertheless. Until one of them came up to him and said,

"My friend and I were just wondering why you have a stuffed toy in your top pocket?" And with that, she reached out to touch it. She jumped in the air when the toy moved and looked at her. After the shock, they all fell about laughing even though neither of the women could believe it.

On another occasion though, a different lady was far from impressed. She had spotted the duckling in his pocket and, as Barrie explained,

"...with a face like a cat having a..."

Now, a face like a what, you may be asking? Before I continue this little story, let me just tell you a little more about Barrie. He is not very politically correct and also has a very colourful use of the English language. Not just with the words, but with the way he uses them. He is one of those people who annoyingly gets away with saying some of the most inappropriate things, but just somehow gets away with it due to the way it was said. He is also absolutely brilliant at embellishing on things and quite regularly turns into Ronnie Corbett, sitting on the end of the chair telling a joke or a story that he has spun into a real tale. He is a larger than life character and in actual fact I think he is like Marmite – you either love him or hate him. Thankfully, the majority of people absolutely love him, and in some cases are drawn to him like a magnet, but there are others who just don't *get* him, and find him too full on and too much.

Anyway, back to the story, let's change his words to "...a face like a defecating cat..." and went storming up to the manager and demanded that the man with a duck in his pocket should be removed from the store as he was a health hazard!

As you can imagine, Star was growing at the rate of knots and soon became too big for the pocket. That wasn't going to hold him back, though. He was still determined to follow his daddy. And that is exactly what happened – he would just follow him. Even when Barrie was working out the back with the other animals, Star stayed close. Interestingly, the other ducks would not acknowledge Star and he them. It was as if Star didn't see himself as a duck and neither did the ducks. We started wondering whether he was, in fact, a human duck.

Whenever Barrie had a nap, which was now becoming at least once a day, Star would have one too – his choice location was on Barrie's head or chest whilst lying on the couch. Star also seemed to enjoy the rugby too, and was getting a genuine taste for real ale – just like his dad! Barrie found this out whilst enjoying a rugby match on the telly, having put his pint down on the floor to hear a slurping noise and Star helping himself! There were a couple of local pubs that enjoyed seeing Star come in and many were fascinated to be so close to a Runner Duck, especially one who liked ale!

It became a real family affair when Barrie went out with his metal detector. Having gained permission from a particular landowner, Barrie would go into the field with the dogs and Star. The dogs loved it and roamed around freely, picking up all the scents with either Drake or Genghis or both managing to find fox poo or the like to roll in somewhere along the line. By the way, if you have never experienced this, it is no laughing matter. I found it funny the first time it happened whilst out walking, until we all got back in the car. The smell is something to behold, even with all the windows open! But Star would stay close to Barrie. You see, Star was a clever duck – he had cottoned on that his dad would go around with this long metal thing and then when it made a noise Barrie would put a marker there. Star would then get inpatient because what he couldn't wait for was for dad to get his spade. As soon as he started digging he just knew there would be plenty of really lovely worms for him to eat. What fun! Not quite as much fun for Barrie though: lots of hard work for no reward as he has yet to find the gold and make his millions!

Now that he was no longer in Barrie's pocket, Star was noticed by passers-by more and more. When Barrie was out and about and couldn't take Star inside with him, people would notice one or both of the Collies sitting in the front seat of the car with a duck next to them. Individuals couldn't help but stop, comment, and take photos. Barrie started taking him out onto the high street with him. That is when people truly started to take note. Individuals in shops looking out couldn't believe their eyes: folks would stop and ask what a goose was doing in Bideford High Street. Some people panicked that maybe a stray duck or a goose or whatever it was, had flown in from somewhere and was stranded. Barrie would then explain that it was his duck, called Star, and he just wanted to be with his dad. I guess it was not surprising that some people thought Star might be a goose as by now all his yellow feathers had gone and he was a striking white, and being a Runner Duck, he had the long neck and obviously stood upright rather than the more traditional duck. He had also started growing a little feather at the back, which curled upwards indicating that he was male.

Star also liked actually going into shops. He became a regular in the local pet shop where Barrie went to buy live meal worms – Star would stroll in larger than life and go and stand behind the counter with the shop assistant. And then there was the local book shop. Barrie had been a frequent shopper there, as despite his big personality, he is also a massive book reader to the point where we could easily open a library with the amount of books he has got through. He thinks there is nothing better than going to bed with a good book, or at least with someone who has read one! No wonder it drew a crowd when Barrie and Star went in there – man and duck standing together scanning the books on the shelves. Other shop owners were keen to help out. The local hairdressers gave us a whole pile of their old towels for his cage/bedroom, which were very gratefully received.

It would be worth pointing out at this time the dynamics in our household had changed. Star was a member of the family, and where once Drake had been top dog, Star was now *top duck*, or at least I am sure that is how the dogs saw it, and Star too for that matter. If I was that way inclined, I could have been as jealous as the dogs obviously were about the relationship forming between duck and man, but I totally understood that they were kindred spirits. Both performers and somehow this was totally meant to be and totally right – despite my earlier reservations. But try telling that to the dogs! Especially ones that already vied for Barrie's attention even before Star came along. Star however, was not fazed by this tug of war for Barrie's attention and affection. If one of the dogs was in his way to getting to his dad, no problem. He would just walk over them to get to him, even if that did mean walking on their head! Genghis and Drake weren't bothered by this, but Meggie wasn't so impressed. She was becoming an old girl now and was not amused!

Chapter Nine

One August day, we went out to a friend's farm where Barrie was training their Collie, with the help of Drake. As it was a miserable wet summer's day, I stayed in the truck with Star on my lap. He had reluctantly stayed in with me as I am sure he would far rather have been out helping his dad. Eventually he settled down and went to sleep – with his neck turned around, laying down his back and tucked into his feathers as he so often did.

When the training had finished, the owner's daughter, Rachel, came back to our house for the afternoon. Wondering how to pass the time, we were messing about on the computer. It was at that point that Rachel suggested that I set up a Facebook profile for Star. I had a Facebook profile myself, but I didn't use it a great deal. I was more of an observer and enjoyed reading other people's posts. When this was suggested I just laughed, and thought it was a daft idea, but nevertheless we started to put one together. Favourite films: Fly Away Home, Charlotte's Web, and Babe. Favourite food: wriggly worms. Favourite pastimes: pooing a lot. Yes, that last one is a bit weird, but they do poo a lot. Thankfully our dogs, and probably most dogs, love duck poo and they happily clean up after Star. Gross but true! Unimaginatively, the profile was named "Star Hayman." I never imagined anyone actually looking at it; it was just a bit of fun. We had a real laugh and the rest of the day passed quickly.

It was now early September and Star was a couple of months old. Barrie received a call from the local newspaper. The reporter told Barrie that they had received many, many calls and emails from the public about seeing a duck on the street, to the point where they were referring to him as the "Bideford Duck," and would we mind if they did an article on them both. This was music to Barrie's ears and he happily agreed.

The local paper comes out on a Thursday. Wednesday evening both Barrie and I were excited, but I was a little more pessimistic, I'd like to call it realistic, and was trying to dumb things down a bit... that it was just a local paper. I was very pleased for Star and Barrie to finally get a bit of recognition for being a bit special and different. It was at that point the phone rang. It was the South West News Agency who had seen the article. We hadn't even seen it as the paper obviously wasn't out yet. The person said there was a lot of interest in this story and would we be okay if ITV came around to interview Barrie and Star in the morning? Barrie was elated. I was a little in shock, and if I'm honest, a little in awe of what might be about to happen.

The next day I went off to work as usual, but with a spring in my step, wondering what might happen next. Barrie went to the shop to get both the daily and local paper, but also in huge anticipation as to what the article would be like. He could sense a difference in the staff from the moment he walked in as they were all smiling at him – for good reason. On the front page was a huge picture of Star *dancing* as a little yellow duckling, and a fantastic write up. Barrie called me straight away to tell me all about it. He couldn't talk for too long as he had to get back for his interview with ITV. I knew that he would be totally at home with this and would be a natural. But what would Star be like?

They filmed them at home with our other animals, on the high street, and even went to the pub. It was such a long day to be at work as I desperately wanted to know how things were going. How was Star doing? Was he okay in front of the camera? If it was ITV, when would they show it on telly? I couldn't wait. I had to call him. But he cut the conversation short as it seemed the phone had been red hot all day and he wanted me off the line in case anyone else was trying to get through. He did have time to say,

"Oh and by the way, we have another reporter coming around shortly! Oh, and another thing, NBC have phoned and they would like to come and film us on Monday."

"Did I hear that right? Did you just say NBC, as in the American channel?"

"Yep. The very same." NBC? I just couldn't believe it.

By the time I got home, he was waiting for me with a cameraman in tow. Could they use my car? They rigged it up with cameras and took off filming with Star on the front seat and Barrie driving around the lanes. It was surreal. I couldn't wait for Barrie to tell me all about the day.

I had actually booked the Friday as a day off work – planned a long time ago to use up my holiday because it was use it or lose it. Barrie came back from collecting his daily paper, but he didn't have one paper: he had about ten. Virtually all the national papers had run the story – the Daily Mail, Express, The Sun, even the Guardian, Telegraph, and Times! Star as a duckling was featured in all of them. What a roller coaster of emotions. All of them also mentioned the Facebook profile, so out of curiosity I switched on the computer to have a look. I hadn't actually managed to log on to the profile before we got a knock on the door. It was our next door neighbour, who said that we had to come and see something. Both Barrie and I had no idea what he was referring to, but got up and went with him anyway. On the way, our neighbour excitedly explained that after seeing all the film crews outside the previous day, he thought he would record the news just in case.

Curiously, both Barrie and I sat on his couch and looked at his huge screen that was currently on pause. He rewound, but it was so fast we didn't take in what it was. Then the lunchtime national ITN news came on. Headlines: Bong (the chime of Big Ben) – Osama Bin Laden has been captured; Bong – President Obama attends an event to mark the anniversary of the falling of the Twin Towers (9/11); Bong – A duck that has taken the country by storm with his master, Barrie Hayman. And there they were: Barrie and Star standing in our front garden!

WHAT? Could this be for real?

For once, even Barrie was speechless. The TV went on fast forward to the ITN newsreaders telling the UK about one man and his duck. And then it went again, to our front garden where Barrie was talking to the camera, with Star in his arms. It then went to them walking down the high street, then to the local pub, and then to the interior of my car with Barrie and Star driving through the local country lanes. We sat there watching in sheer disbelief. Naturally, we asked for it to be rewound several times to let it all sink in. There it was: Osama Bin Laden, the President of the United States, and Barrie and Star Hayman! You just couldn't make it up.

In shock, we headed back home. Could it get any more insane?

Well, yes actually. I went back to the computer to log on to Star's Facebook profile, and there they were – hundreds of friend requests, all saying how they had either read about him or seen him on TV.

The madness didn't end there. The phone rang and it was a local radio station in Birmingham who wanted Barrie to be interviewed live on their show there and then. As a natural, he took it all in his stride. He also passed the phone to Star who did his bit by quacking down the phone. It sounded like it was all going swimmingly until I heard those dreaded words:

"Why don't you ask her yourself?" And with that, the phone was passed to me. In horror, I listened as the presenter – remember this is live on his show – asked me what it was like to be living with a famous duck? To be honest I can't even remember what I replied as I was too much in shock at being thrown unexpectedly and unwillingly into the limelight. I believe it was an okay answer as they were laughing, and as soon as I could, I handed the phone back to Barrie to continue with the interview.

This was all becoming unreal. We knew it wasn't going to stop there because on Monday, NBC was coming to film us.

Chapter Ten

The weekend gave us a little bit of respite, but we were still on a high from the madness of the previous days. Unfortunately I was back at work on the Monday, but NBC wasn't coming until early evening, so with luck I would get home in time. I actually made it home before they got there. They said they had booked into a local hotel for a couple of nights as it could take a while. It is commonly known that it takes time to work with animals or children. They were expecting to do several takes. However, both Star and Barrie were complete naturals. The weather was good so they did the first interview at the front of the cottage. To their surprise, but not ours, they did it in one take. They did more than one shot just because they wanted to get the different camera angles. The cameraman had a field day. He did loads of shots up close to Star and we heard him saying more than once that this was a "Hollywood duck." They then came into the house. NBC was filming in our kitchen! They wanted to see Star's bedroom, and they asked what he ate. Barrie showed them the live meal worms that Star loved so much. Barrie asked the pretty presenter if she would like to feed some to Star. To her credit, she rose to the test and put her hand in, pulled out a couple of wiggly worms and let Star eat them from her hand. I have to confess, as much as I love Star, you will never get me putting my hand in to feed him live worms!

Shortly after, they went off to the local pub to do some filming there. All of the film crews loved the idea that Star was a regular pub-goer. If you ask me, it was just a good excuse to have a pint!

Barrie was back an hour or so later, and he said that the crew had been amazed that they had wrapped already. As with the other film crews, virtually everything had been done in just one take.

Again, we were in a tailspin. Were they serious? A Hollywood duck?

Chapter Eleven

After all the excitement of those mad few days of filming, things settled down a little bit. We were still high as anything knowing that Star would be beamed all over the length and breadth of America, but we wondered what would happen next. Was our fifteen minutes of fame over and done with already?

Now there was a problem with Star's Facebook profile. For some reason, I couldn't log on properly. Having discussed the problem with our IT guy at work, it seemed that the amount of friend requests coming in over such a short period of time had totally blocked it up, and had somehow made it corrupt. Nightmare! I had no idea what to do and the IT guy didn't have any ideas either. What he did show me though, was how to accept the friend requests. That was the only thing I could actually do on this error page. There were so many of them though. There were hundreds of people waiting to be friends with a duck. It was through the endless hours I spent night after night, that we could see the international story unfolding. We knew the moment the story broke in America via NBC, because we had requests coming through from all over America. But it didn't stop there. It seems that both the newspapers and the TV had syndicated our story to their partners across the globe. We could literally see the story rolling around the world over the weeks and months from the requests coming through – Brazil, Argentina, Australia, Japan, China, Vietnam and so many more. Some comments in broken English and others in their own language. At one point through Facebook, I reached out to my pen friend in Italy to see if he could help me interpret some of the Spanish, as they are – to my untrained eye - a very similar language, to find out how they had come across our story.

We didn't seem to have any control on what was happening and that was a bit scary, but it was also pretty incredible that our little Indian Runner Duck from North Devon was now known across the globe.

Chapter Twelve

A few weeks after NBC had carried out their filming, we received a call asking if Barrie and Star would do a TV link up with Morning Sunrise – a live morning TV show in Australia. You can imagine Barrie was absolutely on board with this. Not only would he be in front of the camera again, but also would be beamed across Australia, and therefore his daughter, who still lived there, could see it as well as all of his friends.

He was adamant that I do the interview with him. This was where I came out in cold sweats.

I was reminded of the time years earlier when we travelled down to Cornwall where Barrie was auditioning for a part in Doc Martin (a long-running TV series based in Cornwall). I had stayed talking to the staff while Barrie learned his lines. I was so happy that day, for Barrie to have an audition, and knowing he would be fabulous. I wasn't in the least bit nervous for him. But it was while I was talking to the staff that they suggested I audition too, as they were always on the lookout for extras. As soon as they suggested it, I started shaking like a leaf at the sheer idea. Although I had done some amateur dramatics in my teens and early 20's, this was a totally different ball game. I politely declined, but felt nervous and on edge for the rest of the day. Needless to say, Barrie didn't get the part that day – I hasten to add that this was not necessarily on the back of poor acting skills, but more to his inability to portray a Cornish accent.

And here he was now, absolutely determined that I be with him and Star on live TV. There was a very small part of me that was a little excited at the idea, but another part that was screaming out with fear. If nothing else, I didn't want to let the side down as they were both naturals. I could totally cramp their style by being a nervous wreck, maybe saying the wrong thing or whatever. I really didn't want to do it. Barrie's idea was that we were all in this together, but could I really enhance the experience for everyone by sitting next to him and Star on the sofa? Would I really be of any help? More of a hindrance if you ask me.

Again I had a few days off work, which was great timing following all the excitement and with the forthcoming TV link. It was to be filmed on Friday evening at the BBC studios in the city of Exeter. It had to be late in the evening as it was early morning in Australia. Thursday evening, they sent through the proposed script. Barrie immediately dissed being sent a script. Oh no. Barrie is going to do his own thing. He can't do that, can he? It is live and surely the presenters need to be in control. When I expressed my concern to him, he told me not to worry and that he knew what he was doing. That did absolutely nothing to allay my own fears of the forthcoming experience. That I was doing this at all, let alone with a natural who was intending to do his own thing rather than stick to the script, was a bit intimidating. Also, knowing many of the phrases and statements he usually came out with, I didn't sleep very well that night.

The following morning, Barrie and Star were feeling pretty cool, relaxed, and very excited. I would be lying if I said the same. Yes, I was excited, but was also scared stiff! Our printer had been out of action for a while at home, so I cheekily popped into work, which was only a few miles away, to see if I could get the script printed off there. Despite my trepidation, I was also now secretly getting excited and couldn't wait to talk to my work colleagues about it.

As I walked into the office, all smiles to see my trusted work colleagues, who I knew would be just as excited and chuffed about it all as us, I could sense something was not right. As I was giving them the data stick with the script on it, there was something false about the environment. Couldn't put my finger on it. I could feel that all those in the office were really happy for me, and were more than happy to carry out my cheeky request to print the script for me, but there was something wrong. I just couldn't work out what.

I drove back, script on the seat, but very puzzled. What was all that about? I really didn't understand. Oh well. Put it to the back of the mind for now. I was sure I would get to the bottom of it tomorrow or Monday at the latest. For now, I had to prepare – mentally and practically, for tonight.

I had been home for about half an hour when the post arrived. There amongst the bills, was a letter from work. Puzzled, and with a bad feeling, I opened it up and my world fell apart.

Barrie had Star on his chest and was having a snooze on the couch. I didn't want to wake them. After all, big night tonight, even for pros.

So I went out into the garden. Surely the animals would bring me some comfort?

You see the letter told me that I was being let go, and could I attend a meeting the following week to discuss it.

I worked for a charity that provided schemes and programmes for the unemployed. I had been working there for four years and had worked my way up. Being part of the senior management team meant that I was well aware of the struggles the charity went through with funding. I had helped open and then close several different enterprises the charity had started in order to make money.

I loved working, and work had been my world. I worked hard because I enjoyed it. I got fulfilment from it. Work plus Hayman's Farm, my life had been complete.

Maybe, deep down with all the financial problems and changes the charity had gone through in the last few months, I knew this moment was coming. But today, and the previous few weeks, this had been so far from my mind with everything that had happened with Star and Barrie. It was a total bolt out of the blue and hit me between the eyes. I felt sick. And today of all days.

I looked around at our animals: our little haven. Very proud of where we lived, it was no secret that my wages paid for all this. My world collapsed and I broke down in tears.

Chapter Thirteen

Barrie came out looking for me a short while later with Star waddling closely behind. I tried to hide it from him. The last thing he needed right now was this crisis. I told him that I felt he should do the interview on his own; that I would just cramp his and Star's style. I hoped I would get away with it and tell him in the morning when the interview was over. But Barrie and I had been together too long and knew each other too well. He knew instantly that something was wrong, so I handed him the letter.

He had known how stressful work had been over the last few months, as all of the staff within the charity, including me, had been given a three month redundancy notice only a few months before, but it had been quickly rescinded. This seemed different somehow. More final. We had, in a sense, taken it in our stride the last time, but today I think it was safe to say our stress levels were at an all-time high.

Could we cancel the interview tonight? Neither of us was in the mood to carry it out.

Barrie's initial shock and panic soon turned to anger. Could they not have waited at least for one day before sending this letter, as they knew we had this TV interview tonight? But business is business, I guess. Personal circumstances don't figure in the big scheme of things.

After some further tears and some bordering tantrums, we picked ourselves up. Together we had been through so much already, this one hiccup would not stop us. Bravely we continued to get through the day, ready for tonight. And thankfully, Barrie was now adamant that I wouldn't be on the couch with him and Star. Well, that was one relief!

The interview wasn't until 9.30pm, but true to form, we set off way too early. The trip down was subdued. Rather than our normal chit chat when we were together, we put a CD on – Abba. That would lift our mood a bit! We got some fish and chips when we got into Exeter and then went about trying to find the film studios, asking for directions several times. Barrie was the worst out of the pair of us as he is totally navigationally dyslexic! His idea of how to get somewhere, as I quickly learned on our first ever date together, was don't worry about a map. Just chuck a leftie out of town!

I had envisioned a slightly smaller version of the large, imposing BBC studios in London, but no; a small, single-storied building situated next to a block of flats. And no one was about. Were we in the right place? Walking up close, a tiny sign said BBC. Yes, we were in the right place.

9.10pm, still no one around. What to do? We were both trying to stay calm, and Barrie was trying to get "in the zone" and basically psych himself up for it.

9.15pm – was that a sign of life? A light had gone on inside. We went around to the side where we saw someone through the window and he gave us a wave and signed to go to the front door.

The guy who opened the door introduced himself, and as we in turn did the same, Star waddled through the door. He had never met or even heard of Star and it transpired that when he agreed to do this overtime, he had no idea what to expect. We soon realised that the studios were actually the base for BBC Radio Devon.

He led us down underground to a studio, and started fiddling around with buttons and all sorts. Barrie and I kept looking at each other as we couldn't see any cameras anywhere. Was this a radio interview? Had we got it wrong and it wasn't TV at all? Oh well. Whatever. We were both just trying to keep smiling and enjoying the ride as best we could.

Star meanwhile, seemed totally unfazed and went around the room looking at the shelves full of CDs and special tapes and goodness knows what else that was filling up the room.

The guy looking after us that evening was actually one of the presenters on the radio, but was also producer on some of the other programmes. He was looking a bit perplexed and confused. We were worried. Something was not right. Then the phone rang. It was Australia. He then relaxed, finished the conversation, and now understood. He led us through to another room.

This time, the camera was in situ, directed onto a red couch, which had a backdrop of Exeter Cathedral. He came into his own, back and forth on the phone to the Australian network as they started to get a link going. I soon forgot the stresses from earlier and was fascinated in watching him work, while Barrie and Star made themselves comfortable on the red couch.

A TV came on in front of me and there was my husband and my duck on the screen. And then voices coming through from nowhere – Australian voices. I couldn't keep up with a lot of it as it was one techie talking to another, or rather one producer talking to another. Then another voice came through. It was the director of Morning Sunrise. She spoke to Barrie, explaining that they would be conducting the interview, but could the camera be moved slightly to ensure that both Barrie and Star were in perfect shot. Two other voices came across: the male and female presenters. At first you could hear them just talking with each other, but then they introduced themselves to Barrie.

The countdown began. It was happening. Barrie and I smiled at each other and he gave me a reassuring wink. He was in *the zone* and was ready.

Five, four, three, two, one.

And it began.

I had the script with me and they started asking the first question. But as promised, Barrie soon went off piste and took the conversation away from what was scripted and the presenters were on the back foot. While I squirmed, Barrie visually relaxed and started to have some fun. He was now in control and soon had the presenters laughing.

He recalled how Star started out in his pocket and went to the shops with him, but again, totally went off the script. Of course, Barrie mentioned the woman in the supermarket.

"...who had a face like a..." Gulp. Here we go. Be careful, Barrie. You are on live, family TV.

"...defecating cat..." Phew, that was close. Good boy. Keep it clean!

"What is so special about Star?" the presenter asked.

"Well, he doesn't sing, do somersaults, or play the piano, but he is a very special duck. He comes with me everywhere, even to the pub. He just loves real ale, and loves watching rugby too. My wife, Sue, also enjoys the rugby, but only from the waist down."

"So what does your wife think about having a duck in the house?"

"She has been fine with it all. However, she drew the line at him coming into the bed with us. So with a few alterations, Sue is now happily living in the goose house!"

And so it went on.

Knowing Barrie, what he says and how he says it, there were times when I had my head in my hands, anticipating what was coming, and worried if he was going to be offensive or be politically incorrect or use some naughty language. At the last minute, he would always twist it somehow so it was totally acceptable. He had the presenters in fits. I was also in fits at times, but mine was more laughter out of sheer relief than because it was actually funny. After all, I had heard all this many times before.

They started bringing the interview to a close. Barrie said,

"If you are as fit as you sound, bonny lass, then you must be the duck's nuts!" Laughter came from everywhere at this point as the producer, director, and crew were now back on the line to announce it was a wrap. I realised then, that Barrie had carried out this interview completely blind. I thought he could see the people he was talking to, but no. He could only hear them like I could.

The director was still laughing and thanking Barrie. We could also hear the presenters in the background saying that that was the first time they had been very happy to come in early to pre-record an interview. So not quite live then, but near enough.

After having some photos taken whilst on the red couch, we came away buzzing. Again Barrie and Star had proved complete naturals and it was a great success.

Star had taken the whole experience all in his stride as we knew he would. To be fair, he was also a little shy too, but very well behaved. Certainly didn't move from Barrie's side throughout the whole interview.

The stresses from earlier that day could wait. This was our moment and we were going to enjoy it.

Chapter Fourteen

We stayed on a false high from the success of the interview throughout the weekend. We could visualise Nicky, Barrie's daughter, and his grandson Ethan, along with Barrie's friends all watching. Messages soon started coming in - same old Hayman. Most of his friends, including me, knew him as and referred to him as Hayman as opposed to Barrie. Not changed a bit; cheeky chappy; aged a bit, but not really changed, etc.

Friend requests also continued to come through on Facebook. It was so frustrating not being able to fully use this site, but I was still letting in sometimes hundreds each day. People from all over the world: male, female, all ages. Some were doing it through the novelty of being friends with a duck; others were sharing stories of their own ducks and animals, and still others were just interested and excited about Star in general with acknowledgement and recognition at being a special duck.

However, the black cloud was still there. I still had to go in for the redundancy meeting. With insight to the potential problems of the charity, maybe I should have already been looking for another job? But I hadn't. I'd been caught out. What were we going to do?

Despite now having a famous duck that was literally known throughout the world through one media form or another, we had not financially gained in any way. Everything we had done had been without any fee, and we had absolutely no control on what was sent where or to whom. With redundancy looming, desperation set in so I reached out. Naively I contacted a well-known publicist to the rich and famous. Could they help with the media in any way, to ensure we were not exploited, but also to maybe gain something in some way? Not surprisingly, we were given a polite but to the point email, stating that they were very sorry but we were on our own with this one.

The day arrived. I arranged to have my colleague, Kim, in the meeting with me. So nervous and having no idea what to expect, I prepared for the worst.

I was back home within a couple of hours.

Barrie was nervously waiting for me as I walked through the door. Resigned for the inevitable, but to his surprise, and mine too at the time, although my role had now been made redundant, they didn't want to lose me and had offered me a different position. I hadn't accepted as I wanted to discuss it with Barrie first.

We soon unanimously agreed to take the job being offered. Less money, slightly less responsibility, but it was still a job and in actual fact it was the same job, but with all the bits that I hadn't really enjoyed or got real job satisfaction taken away. So it wasn't so bad after all.

We still had to tighten our belts, though, but at least we were safe. All was okay. The cottage, its occupants, and Hayman's Farm were not going anywhere.

The weeks that followed were relatively quiet. The phone no longer rang asking for interviews and nothing further was in the diary. Things were settling down at work and Facebook friends and messages continued to roll in.

It gave us a bit of breathing space. The roller coaster had stopped doing the loop the loop and was now just coasting along at a reasonable and manageable pace. The two-week madness was becoming simply a memory; a fantastic and exciting one, but just a memory now and nothing more.

So, what was it all about? Was that truly our fifteen minutes of fame all now done and dusted? Barrie and I continued to question this as the days passed.

In the local paper, I spotted an advert from a casting agent asking for people to come to an open day audition to be on their books, to potentially later appear in various different TV and film productions in the area. We thought we would go along and have a look. Maybe we could enrol both Barrie and Star. When we arrived, the queue as we suspected, was leading out the door. Loads and loads of people had come along as there were no required acting skills; they just wanted people of all ages mainly for extra/walk on parts. As I dutifully joined the back of the queue, I knew this would be a very frustrating time as Barrie was rubbish with waiting and queues at the best of times. However, I soon realised I was on my own. Looking towards the front of the queue, I noticed Barrie go through the door – it seems Star was no good at waiting either and walked straight in! With huge embarrassment, and apologising all the way, I also majorly queue jumped and found Star was soon the centre of attention. There was some sort of system on the go where you filled in a form, then went on to the next bit where you were measured, and then waited your turn to be photographed. Star was already standing by the photographer! To my relief, no one seemed at all miffed about Star's blatant act of queue jumping and attention seeking, and he was photographed next. I, meanwhile, spoke to one of the organisers, took a blank application form from them and left them with Barrie's Curriculum Vitae, which outlined all his commercials, films, and TV acting work throughout the years. We were in and out of there within about ten minutes.

The problem was, although no one was knocking on our door with any further offers – despite being told he was a "Hollywood duck," Star was in our face all day every day. We knew absolutely and categorically that he was not a normal duck. Never was and never would be. So why was he here? Why had Star been given to Barrie? The bond they had was so strong, there had to be a reason for it. What was the purpose? What should we be doing?

As I mentioned before, we had not benefited financially in any way from all the media attention. The money would have been very gratefully received, because living on one wage and a basic pension was no easy feat when you had Hayman's Farm to feed, but we knew there was more to Star than just being a potential money generator. But what was it?

Even though I was used to seeing Star being around the house as a member of the family, I still occasionally found myself stop what I was doing and watch him now and again, just like everyone else. The way he would groom himself was of interest. He would give himself a thorough wash from his water dish, as we would do if we were having a strip wash, just without the flannel and soap. The way he ate erratically, like it was his only meal with the corn going all over the place, tap, tap, tapping away with his beak like a woodpecker with bark on a tree. When all three of the dogs were sitting, waiting, looking at me patiently to give them a treat, Star would be standing next to them, looking at me, waiting for his treat, too. The way he slept: sometimes on one leg balancing on the arm of the sofa, with his head turned around and laying across his back, with his beak buried in his feathers. Or literally flying, or I suppose gliding would be more apt as he can't fly, off the arm of the sofa half way across the room to catch up with his dad who got up to go to the loo or to go to another room. The way his webbed feet made a pitter patter noise on the wooden floor as he walked along. This was all so very endearing.

However, he was also a little rascal, too. Just like a toddler, he would poke his beak at anything that was at his level – keys, pens, phones on the coffee table. He would move them around and even nudge them off the table, not to mention winding up the dogs! Paperwork: he just loved that. There were times I went into work red-faced, having to explain that my duck had eaten my homework!

The question still remained:- what happens next? Barrie and I had endless discussions about this. Maybe we needed to stop thinking selfishly. We eventually came to a conclusion. A time when Barrie would forever more refer to as the "epiphany moment." Star was not given to us to make money and have stardom for ourselves. He was presented to use as a platform for others to appreciate, to smile and find comfort in. Not only was Star a human duck, he was actually the people's duck. He had proved to be a natural in front of the camera and with the media. But what had brought all this attention in the first place? He liked people. He liked being with and around people. And the people liked him. He had brought a smile to everyone who met him. No matter what age, what background, what was going on in their lives, they all found pleasure in seeing Star.

So with this in mind, how could we and how should we take this forward?

We all know about dogs that go into hospitals and care/nursing homes. It is often referred to as animal therapy. We had thought about it years ago with our first dog Molly, due to her lovely temperament. Maybe we could do this with Star? I remembered there was a Children's Hospice in the area from dealings with them through work. Maybe they would be interested in meeting Star? We were in agreement. We would approach the Children's Hospice South West.

But we wanted him to look his best. We knew he cleaned himself up pretty well. Even after he insisted on going into the muddiest puddles he could find! We wanted something more. Barrie produced a tie that had gathered dust at the back of the wardrobe. It had a big picture of Donald Duck on.

"What about this?" he asked.

"I can cut it up so it fits," he added. It was too long and despite the fact he never wore it, it would be a shame to butcher it. This gave me a different idea. I retrieved one of Barrie's handkerchiefs, folded it diagonally and tied it around Star's neck.

"Cowboy duck," I pronounced. But Barrie wasn't convinced and headed off upstairs coming back with one of his bow ties. Again, something he had never worn. Can't even remember why we had bought it in the first place and even more why we still had it! He tied it around Star's neck and bingo! The look was complete. Star wasn't too impressed though, and spent the next few minutes running around in circles backwards, pecking at it with his beak. Then he settled down and admitted defeat. It looked like I had some sewing to do.

So with Star looking dapper in his newly sewn, made to measure bow tie, Barrie and Star set off to the Children's Hospice South West. We had no idea what the reception would be like, but Barrie had to give it a try. It felt like it was somehow their destiny. With the help of my directions, they found Little Bridge House, the head office of the Children's Hospice. It was a nice, new looking building, set back in the heart of a housing estate. Feeling a little nervous, he went into the reception and introduced himself asking if they would be interested in meeting Star. The Community Fundraiser, Emma, was called out, and after hearing what Barrie had to say, announced that they would love to meet him. With that, Barrie collected Star from the car.

Well, who couldn't resist a duck with a bow tie? They were smitten. Barrie told them what he had in mind and they took him up on the offer straight away, inviting them both there and then to go through and meet the children. As if Star had been there before, he led the way. Waddling down the corridor, he only stopped to wait for the next code-locked door to be opened. It was meal time so those who were able, were in the dining room.

As soon as Star waddled through the door, faces lit up, both adults and children alike. Barrie was immediately struck by how relaxed everything was. He had no idea who were staff and who were family members. Many of the children were in wheelchairs or assisted in some way. Despite the fact that many of those in the room were very seriously ill, all acknowledged the presence of Star in their own way.

Some of the children's siblings were there and came over to see Star, along with some of the more able-bodied children. Barrie carefully explained to them that Star doesn't like being handled. If they wanted to touch Star, to go around to the front of him and put their hand out gently and stroke his beak.

He turned away to talk to some of the adults and address the other children who had not been able to move towards Star. When he looked back, he saw that one of the youngsters was actually cuddling Star. And then a different child started stroking him as if he was a cat. Was this for real? Barrie thought he knew and understood almost everything about Star, but this was a totally different side to him. It was as if Star understood exactly where he was and what he needed to do. If Barrie previously had any doubts about bringing him along, they were now truly dispelled.

He appreciated that this part of the hospice was like the inner sanctum. Apart from the children residing there, their families and obviously the staff who worked there, many people wouldn't see this. It was very emotional, uplifting, heartbreaking, and if Barrie was honest, at times a little awkward. It seemed though, that Star was not in the least affected by any of this. It was as if he had a job to do and he got on and did it. He took it all in his stride, and the children and adults alike loved him for it.

Barrie came away elated. Looking at Star, he was sure he was waddling just that little bit taller maybe?

By the time I arrived home from work, Barrie was desperate to tell me all that had happened. He was full of emotion too, and I am sure he wouldn't mind me telling you he cried his heart out. The children, their families, the staff, Little Bridge House; it had touched his soul and his mind was made up. The Children's Hospice was going to play a major part in his and Star's life. It really was their destiny. This was why Star was here – to make a difference to people's lives.

Chapter Fifteen

Throughout the weeks that followed, Barrie continued to take Star wherever he went. Locals were getting used to seeing him and visitors to the area would stop and take photos. Many of them had seen him on TV or read about him. Wearing his bow tie whenever he went outdoors, there was no mistaking Star for a stray. It was while Barrie was recounting the days' events to me one evening, it occurred to him that he met so many people; maybe he could take advantage of that. What if he were to ask the Children's Hospice to give them one of their collection tins? Maybe he could put this attention to good use and raise both money and awareness in the process?

So the next time Barrie and Star went to the Hospice's head office, which was not long after that initial visit as they were just as keen as Barrie was for them to return, he asked if they would give him something he could collect money in. With that, they got him a bucket, a smaller cylindrical collecting container, and threw in some T-shirts for good measure, all with the Children's Hospice's logo emblazoned on the outside.

Now they were in business. Whether they were on the high street, in the pub, or on the beach, they took the collection container with them. The first time he went out onto the street with Star carrying the Hospice collection tin, he stood to the side with Star standing next to him. People dutifully came up to them and put money in. The more times they went out, the more their confidence grew and realised to their delight, that the tin got filled up far too quickly. The tin was soon ditched and the bucket was brought out.

One particular trip, Barrie and Star were driving towards town, the dogs in the car with them. They approached the main roundabout, which was traffic light controlled. Whilst Barrie was waiting for the light to change a police car drew up to the side of them. Barrie noticed the two officers in the car looking at him strangely and wondered what the problem was. Meanwhile, the lights changed so Barrie pulled away. He didn't get very far when he saw the police flash their lights and indicated for him to pull over. What was wrong? Did he have a light out or something? The officer came to Barrie's window all smiles and explained that the last thing they had expected to see when they had pulled up at the lights was a duck sitting on the front seat staring back at them! They said they needed to get a photo as proof for their sergeant on getting back to base, that they weren't drinking on the job! Barrie was so relieved. He had totally forgotten that it was a bit of an unusual sight to see a duck on the front seat of the car.

Unfortunately, it wasn't all sunshine and flowers when Barrie went out with Star. There was one very hair raising moment when they were all out at the beach. The dogs were happily running up and down the sand, in the sea, out of the sea. Racing and chasing each other while making friends with other dogs and their owners. Star partly watched in envy to be one of the pack, but also glad to be close to his dad, whilst having fun digging out the sea worms, and enjoying the sand beneath his webbed feet. Although it was nearly winter, it wasn't raining and the wind wasn't strong. It was, with the right clothing, pleasant. As was becoming the norm, people were coming up to talk to Barrie. Some of them, like the pre-Star days, were to compare notes on the dogs. But mostly it was about Star. On this particular day, a lady came up to them, very animated and excited to finally meet the duck she had read so much about. She had a puppy with her and although he was on a lead, to be on the safe side Barrie picked Star up. This was after Star had given him the run around for a bit. The lady was keen to hear and see more about what she had read, but the puppy could not contain himself any longer. He just had to do it. Before anyone had a chance to react, the pup had jumped up and grabbed Star. Taken completely unawares, Barrie struggled to keep hold of Star and felt him being pulled down. Then the pulling stopped. Star was still in his arms, but there was blood and lots of it. There was also screaming. Barrie could only assume that it was coming from the owner of the puppy as to the high pitch. But he couldn't be sure that he wasn't shouting or screaming himself. Had the dog just taken Star's leg off?

Without giving a second thought to the puppy or its owner, Barrie ran for the car, calling Drake, Genghis and Meggie to follow suit. Thankfully as Collies, they are actually quite brainy and realised something wasn't right and came running after him. They all piled into the car and Barrie put his foot down heading for the veterinary surgery. Even though it was only a few miles away, it was that bit too far at that moment in time. Barrie didn't want to waste any time and possibly broke a few speed limits during that near-on fifteen minute drive. On reaching his destination he ran in with Star and seeing the blood, they managed to find a vet to see them straight away.

After several heart-stopping moments the vet announced that both legs were still there. No bones had been broken, but a large chunk of muscle had been removed. They would need to operate on Star and get him stitched back up. Following a lot of convincing from the veterinary staff, and with great reluctance, Barrie left Star there and came home. By the time I arrived home, Barrie was a bit of an emotional wreck. Knowing that anaesthetics on any animal were risky, let alone on a five month old Indian Runner Duck, I had no words that I could give of reassurance. Just cuddles had to suffice.

A few long hours later, the vets phoned to say the operation had been a success. Star was coming around well. They even managed to make us smile when they recounted the story of how many vets it had taken to come up with what could only be described as a nappy due to the position of the wound: around the top of the leg and bottom area. We could go and collect him within the hour. An hour? No way. We were in the car straight away.

They weren't kidding about the nappy! But he was okay, a little subdued perhaps, but alive. The nappy didn't stay on very long. It seemed Star didn't appreciate being treated like a baby, almost as if it hurt his pride or something. So he immediately set about trying to remove it. Despite our efforts, it was off within a couple of hours. We tried all sorts as a substitute: an old T-shirt cut up; you name it. In the end we had to admit defeat knowing that we were taking a risk from the wound getting infected, but Star wasn't exactly helping us to help him.

Thankfully it was all okay, and the wound didn't get infected. Although it looked nasty for a while, with regular visits to the vets, it eventually healed.

But the trips to the beach stopped, certainly as far as Star was concerned. Whenever Barrie took the dogs for a run, Star had to settle for being left in the car and could only watch and not take part. We had learned a valuable lesson; not all dogs were friendly to ducks! What we didn't realise at the time was that Star had also learned a lesson. There was no way humans were going to make him wear a nappy again. From that day on, whenever Star encountered a dog, usually in the street, he wouldn't take any messing. Barrie would forever more witness Star going for dogs that could eat him for breakfast, but in fact would run away and cower behind their owner or be chased down the street. The same went for pigeons or any other animals that deemed to get into his space.

Star continued to cause a stir wherever he went. When Barrie and Star were walking down the high street, bucket in hand, Star would quite regularly just walk into a shop, seemingly at random. Barrie would run in after him very apologetic. But no one seemed to mind. Maybe Star had a sixth sense and felt there was someone in that shop, whether they be staff or browsers, who just needed a pick-me-up. And he was there to give them something to smile about. He still continues to do it to this day. Unfortunately, we can't ask him to explain this. We could also be totally reading too much into this and that in actual fact he is just a duck who loves the attention. After all, as well as walking into the shops he will also walk up to small crowds, or a small group huddled together and go and stand in the middle of them, just looking up at them, waiting to be noticed. Yes, you're right. He's probably just an attention seeking diva!

There have also been some useful people who have met Star. Just before Christmas, not long after Star had started his regular visits to the Hospice and begun their fundraising, Barrie met and spoke to a guy called Tony, a professional cameraman who would just love to film Star in action. So over the next few weeks Barrie and Star were in Heaven as they were again performing in front of the camera. Tony was not only a fantastic cameraman, but was also an absolute whiz with all the technology. Getting it all uploaded onto the Internet, he set up a YouTube page specifically for Star: starduckonline. But in order to get any visitors onto the site, we wanted some interesting footage, not just filming them out at work on the street collecting money.

Barrie and Star had been invited along to a children's Christmas party. It was at a nursery school so all the children were pre-school age. Some were in fancy dress. Others wore mini suits and best dresses. Both Star and the children thoroughly enjoyed themselves. For Star's part, he was mixing with people who were on his level, literally. None of them were towering over him. In Star's eyes he was one of them. For the kid's part, they talked to him, played with him and just like in the Hospice, were able to cuddle and stroke him. And better still, I didn't have to visualise this from what Barrie told me afterwards. I could see it all for myself on his YouTube page. The interaction between duck and toddler was amazing. Luckily, this wasn't going to be the last time we would see this as it continues each and every week, with both regulars and strangers alike with Star and the little people.

Sometimes after a thirsty day of "work," Barrie and Star would go into the pub and have a cheeky pint. Star loves his real ale and would regularly tuck into Barrie's pint. Dipping his beak into the glass, then lifting his head up and back making a little gargling noise as it went down. So many times Barrie noticed that those who witnessed this in the pub couldn't help but text home to say there was a duck in the pub drinking beer. Only seemingly to receive a curt reply back saying that they had obviously had far too much to drink and it was time to go home. On receiving this they would then have to take a photo as proof that it was not beer goggles talking.

The landlord of one particular pub was a very good singer and had a karaoke machine. When Barrie and Star went in there it was pretty much always off peak and therefore only a few regular punters were there. Quite often the landlord would be singing on the machine. And Star loved it. It was like he was being serenaded. Barrie introduced the landlord to Tony and between them they concocted a plan: filming the landlord singing to Star. As Christmas was just around the corner, the song choice was unanimous: White Christmas. Not with Bing Crosby, but with the landlord. This time, Barrie found himself relegated to film crew and props master as the filming took place. It didn't all go according to plan as Star did have a few diva moments and seemed to be quite attracted to the tinsel, but Tony kept the filming going the whole time. The finished article on YouTube was fantastic: great singing; great scenes of heavy snowfall taken from the previous year; and great footage of Star being cute through the serenading, but also being naughty and trying to trash the set. It was a shame that it was just that bit too close to Christmas to get it ready as a CD stocking filler.

Drake was also filmed at work. Not rounding up sheep, but rounding up the ducks. Barrie did this quite regularly not only to keep the ducks fit, but also to let Drake work. The novelty was that Star was there the whole time by Barrie's side. Star wouldn't dream of getting himself rounded up by Drake or any other Collie. That didn't mean Drake hadn't tried in the early days. Barrie had tried to use Drake to round Star up when he was being a little annoying and not ready to come in, but Star very quickly showed he was having none of it. By now though, this was understood and he was part of the supervision team. Watching it all happening, probably in Star's own mind he was actually helping with the round up. After all, he wasn't actually a duck himself was he?

Barrie had used Drake to work both the geese and the ducks from the very beginning of Hayman's Farm having been given the idea when he first saw the ducks being worked by a Collie at the local tourist attraction. For fun, Barrie had gone a stage further by putting up some props around the garden so they would have to be shepherded through and over things, and then into the pond. There were two Bed and Breakfasts in the hamlet and quite regularly passers-by would stop to watch Drake working the animals, with Star standing by Barrie's side the whole time.

Chapter Sixteen

Christmas was a quiet affair in the Hayman household. The only difference this time compared to previous years was not just three dog snouts nosing at the present opening, but a beak in there, too. Just like them – and all toddlers throughout the land – Star just loved the wrapping paper. Of course we had to make sure he had a present just like each of the dogs. For him it was some smoked oysters. He really liked cheese and tomatoes too, but that wouldn't have been a very special present, would it?

On New Year's Eve we received a call late in the afternoon from Little Bridge House. Could Star come in as they had had a special request from one of the children's family? Although we had made plans for the evening, Barrie didn't hesitate. I came along, too. It was the first time I had been along to the Hospice with Barrie and Star, and although I had some idea of what to expect, I was a little nervous.

When we got there we were led through to the Chapel to where most of the children were waiting. The young boy whose family had requested the visit, was there in his wheelchair with his portable DVD. On seeing Star, his face lit up and the DVD was ignored. I was now seeing Star at work properly for the first time. He walked past each and every person and then stood in the middle of the room, preened himself and then slowly walked to the little boy as if he knew exactly who had asked for him to come in. Without any fuss or giving him the run around, Barrie was able to pick Star up and put him on the little boy's lap. The boy laughed and laughed, as did everyone else. The parents were laughing and crying in equal measure. I just sat there in awe of what I was witnessing. After a little while, Star was put back down and he again made his way around the room. Stopping, and in his own way, connecting with each and every one of them in the room. There was one young girl who had met him before, but had not got too close as she was too frightened. But she was gaining confidence and she started interacting with Star too. Again, Star allowed the children to hold him, stroke him, touch him, do whatever they liked and he stood there bold as brass, happy to be making them all smile. As we were leaving, the little girl who had once been so nervous of him was helped out and walking behind him. She actually gave him a little nudge with her foot to move Star along. Although a small gesture, we all knew that this was a real leap forward for this little lady, and Star was certainly none the worse for it. One could wonder whether he knew what he was doing and had staged this for her benefit?

I was very touched by that visit and was taken by surprise when later that evening I cried. I now totally understood why Barrie had been so passionate and adamant in their dedication to the Children's Hospice South

West.

It was not long after this visit that the Children's Hospice made Star their official mascot. Star also received an ID badge with his photo on it. He was an official fundraiser. Obviously, Barrie was to wear this around his neck rather than Star as it might clash with his bow tie!

Chapter Seventeen

That winter was not a really cold one, but an extremely wet one. It rained and rained, so much so that Hayman's Farm was more like Hayman's Lake. Even though the geese and ducks could swim, even they were not impressed as there was very little grass. It was just a soggy mud bath.

Despite being given permission for animals when we first moved in, and despite the fact that we couldn't control the weather, the agent for our cottage was not happy with the "mud bath." On their all too regular inspections they continued to point this out to us as a problem that we needed to address. In addition to this, we had an elderly neighbour whom we had previously got on very well with. He was almost like a father figure to Barrie, but it seemed for some reason now he had decided that he no longer wanted us to be living there any more. Unfortunately, he continually caused us problems by phoning the owner of our cottage who was someone he had known for a long time. To which we would then almost immediately receive a visit by the agent. In actual fact we had done nothing wrong. When I say "us" by the way, I mean Barrie as I was invariably at work when these unexpected and unwelcome visits took place. This took its toll on Barrie and our haven, in his eyes, was slowly becoming hell.

The only thing that kept Barrie going and in actual fact got him out of the front door, was going out with Star. We started to count up the money before giving it to the Children's Hospice. They were collecting anything from £100 to nearly £400 in one collection over the space of a couple of hours. It was incredible. People were giving for two reasons: one for the Children's Hospice, as everyone is touched by that in some way, whether through direct experience or just grateful that they had never had to use their service. And two, Star. People could not get enough of seeing him. Not only with people who had read about him or seen him on TV and had come to Devon on the off-chance hoping to see him, but many locals and regulars. They loved to meet Star, but also to meet Barrie as well. Many of the locals were older members of the community who even now save up their small change, ready to give. The toddlers and their parents too and even teenagers found Star cool. We think this had something to do with the fact that Russell Howard - a comedian on TV who presents a regular show based on the current news – had shown footage of Barrie and Star. Albeit taking the "mick" out of them both, but in a light hearted and fun way.

Unfortunately, there were others who were not so happy to see Barrie and Star in the street. They came from several different places. There was one guy who Barrie and Star regularly saw when they were out in the high street. Each time he put his loose change into the bucket. However, on one occasion he asked Barrie,

"What are you collecting for this time?" Barrie, a bit taken aback, explained that as always, they were raising money for the Children's Hospice. At this, the guy asked him,"Why are you collecting for the same charity? Surely there are other charities out there you could also be collecting for that are of a more worthy cause?"

Barrie couldn't believe what he was hearing, but the guy hadn't finished.

He continued on. "What is the point of having all this money spent on them when they are going to be dead soon anyway?"

Barrie was flabbergasted at this. He was born shortly after the end of the Second World War when Hitler had taken children who would have been in a hospice today, to be exterminated along with the Jewish population. Thank God we live in a different era. Every life is precious no matter how short. Barrie can't remember what his response was to this man. Probably a good job too, as I doubt I would have been able to put it into print!

Animal rights: Barrie and Star were almost attacked in the street by some people claiming that Barrie was being cruel by making a duck walk the streets. He had heard this many times before and continually since. Each time Barrie would calmly explain how Star actually enjoyed doing this and if he didn't he wouldn't hang around. It was not like he was kept on a lead or anything. Star was certainly not doing this by force. But there was one occasion where a lady became particularly aggressive, openly claiming she was part of animal rights. She actually tried to attack Barrie both verbally, by shouting and swearing, and physically, too. It was the local people of Bideford who surrounded Barrie to protect him while a shop owner, who had seen the commotion, managed to pick Star up and take him to safety. The local CCTV had picked this up and the police were there very quickly, but not quick enough to catch the lady who had caused the commotion as she had fled the scene. As you can imagine, Barrie was pretty shaken up afterwards. He did manage to smile at the fact that the shop owner who had *rescued* Star from the situation, was in fact the local butcher! Everyone chuckled at the irony of that. As this hadn't been the first time, Barrie went to the nearby RSPCA with Star to get their view. They fully supported Barrie and Star and actually put out a statement to clarify this when the story hit the local press. They still have people coming up to them claiming to be animal rights, but thankfully not with the same amount of aggression as that occasion.

Buskers (who are entertainers of any genre, on the street with a cap or instrument case in front of them to collect money from passers-by for their own means): Although they all got on well with Barrie, they were also gutted to see him and Star as they knew they might not collect as much themselves that day. But Barrie built up a good relationship and understanding with them and they usually managed to sort something out, like a different part of the street or whatever.

And then there were the other charities: most of them were great. The majority of them were volunteers themselves who had also given up their own time to collect for a worthy cause. Many were just as in awe as most people were about meeting Star, and usually put money in the bucket, too. Those who weren't so happy were those in charge of the collection and quite often paid members of staff for that particular charity. They frequently made sure Barrie knew their displeasure at seeing them out on the street. Some of them got pretty heated and in some cases, spiteful. There were several altercations in the street where some of them literally shouted at Barrie. Again though, the people who understood and appreciated what they were doing and loved Star surrounded them both, and Barrie found that he didn't need to say anything. The people would just move him and Star out of the way whilst others had a showdown with the perpetrators. It seemed a very sorry state of affairs and a real shame that Star could bring such joy to the majority of the people, but others just wouldn't accept what they were doing. It seemed that it was those same people who, in the name of charity, put in calls to the councils. The absolute minority who complained about Barrie and Star being out on the street were those who called.

Barrie is a tough cookie and stubborn with it. He would not back down. Having said that, I was the one who was privately picking up the pieces behind closed doors with the effect this was having on him: the trouble with the neighbour so Barrie spent less and less time with the animals; the regular visits from the agent; and then being harassed on the streets, too. He was becoming ill. All the while he was out performing with Star either on the street, where he was still raising so much money, or going to the Hospice visiting the children, he appeared to the outside world as a real happy-go-lucky chap. Many people thought the absolute world of him. But once back home, door closed, he would totally go into his shell and become a nervous wreck. On coming home from work in the evenings I would have no idea what to expect. I was worried that he was close to having a breakdown.

Chapter Eighteen

To make matters worse, we received a letter from the council. Unless Barrie acquired a licence, he and Star could no longer raise money on the streets. And if they were caught again, the council would have no option but to take them to court.

What?

What the hell was all that about?

Well, it seems that prior to this Barrie had been approached by the council whilst out with Star on the high street. The council worker was a really nice guy and very apologetic, but said that in order to keep doing this Barrie would need to apply for a licence. A discussion ensued between them both about what Barrie and Star actually did on the high street. Surely all they were doing was entertaining the local people? The council worker privately agreed.

An occurrence the previous week now made sense: whilst out collecting Barrie had noticed a huddle of smartly dressed people standing outside a charity shop. They were watching him and Star and obviously talking about them as they kept pointing towards their direction several times. Barrie thought he actually recognised at least one of them, but couldn't place them. Following the discussion with the friendly council worker, it seemed that the councils pursuit of Barrie was on the back of another charity making a complaint. Barrie realised now that the person he recognised had been the CEO of this other charity.

Although I was in complete agreement with Barrie, I wanted to do the right thing so I completed the application form they had enclosed as best I could. The problem was though that there wasn't a box to tick for a duck! I tried to explain on the form that they were not only raising money for charity, but they were also entertainment and essentially a tourist attraction in their own right. We knew this first hand as Barrie heard people all the time on their mobiles telling whoever to come down because Star was there. We knew that the high streets were dying at the hand of the big out of town supermarkets. Barrie and Star were pulling crowds back in. Not only that, we lived in a tourist area. So it was not just the locals who were donating, and yet the money was being given to a local charity.

But despite trying to explain all this on the form, as suspected the application was rejected and we were invited to re-apply again.

Barrie was having none of it and refused to do it again suspecting it would no doubt be rejected again. Besides, if he had been successful in being issued a licence, then it would limit him to where and when he could go out with Star. He would be limited to one visit per month to whichever town, with countless separate applications having to be made to all the different town and district councils, requesting a specific day one month in advance. Well, that didn't suit at all. For one, we live in the UK where the weather is totally unpredictable. And two, his health was not great. Therefore, he couldn't plan ahead where and when he was going out.

In addition to that, Star and Barrie were not collectors. In actual fact they were buskers who happened to give their busking money to charity. There was a difference, wasn't there?

The councils however, seemingly couldn't see what a benefit Star and Barrie were to the community. They would not acknowledge that they were not only well-loved by the local people, but also bringing some life back into the high streets.

A man was sent out on behalf of the council several more times over the weeks that followed and Barrie realised "the plank," as he now affectionately called the council worker named on the letters we received, would not come to see him in the flesh. One day when he was out and about with Star, tap, tap on his shoulder. As he turned around, he had to look up. Bless him; most people are taller than him at only five foot four.

"Hello, Barrie. I'm here on behalf of the plank!" And there was this guy looking down at him.

Gulp!

You see, Barrie is not backward in coming forward. During all his visits to the various different towns over the past few weeks, everyone who came up to see Star were told about the plank and how he and his team were trying to get them to complete the application form that is a one size fits all, which is no good when the subject matter is a duck.

The guy was pleasant enough, despite his colleague now infamously being renamed, and urged Barrie to re-apply for the licence.

Of course, Barrie dug his heels in and continued to refuse, much to my concern not only for the hassle and unwelcome negativity, but also for his health with the stress this was all causing.

It was while they were out collecting on the street that they were approached by an art collector. She was arranging a gallery in aid of the Royal National Lifeboat Institution (RNLI). They always had a showcase picture that was raffled off at the end of the three day event for the charity. Could Star be the subject of this showcase picture? Of course. Aside from the excitement of a portrait of Star, Barrie was more than happy to be helping to raise money for this charity, having spent so much of his life in Australia in, on, or under the sea. He had great respect for them.

So Barrie took Star to meet with the artist who took lots of photos from varying different angles and was just as excited as we were.

The invite to the Art Collection arrived and Barrie said to me,

"Grab a bath, have a shave, and scrub your tooth. I am going to be presenting you to a Countess. We are going to the Castle Hill Estate," which was a lovely mansion nearby owned by relatives to the Royal Family. We were so excited, not just about going to such a prestigious event, but also to see our duck as an oil painting. In addition to being the subject of the showcase picture, Star also had another role for the evening: to meet and greet the guests on arrival. Due to his starring role we made sure that Star had a black bow tie for the occasion. It was a prestigious event after all.

Once Star had successfully said hello to each and every person on arrival, the Countess herself then did the initial address to all the attendees. Star however, was not going to be upstaged whether she was a Countess or not. He went and stood right in front of her, taking centre stage. And as she spoke, he made sure that everyone was under no illusion as to who the real star was! Thankfully, the Countess saw the funny side, even buying a raffle ticket to be in with a shot of winning the painting!

Star had a fantastic time showing off his black bow tie to everyone. He appeared to take his role very seriously. I think he also approved of the portrait. Barrie and I did, too. The artist had really caught Star's spirit, as well as a fantastic likeness including Star's favourite blue felt bow tie.

Another event Star and Barrie went to was a totally different affair. They were invited along with the Children's Hospice fundraising team to a home game at Exeter Football Club. No one knew how this would go. We knew Star loved people, but this would be thousands of supporters making a lot of noise. As usual we shouldn't have worried. Star stole the show. Throughout the game, Star walked around the stands mingling with the supporters while they watched the game. The noise, the people, again didn't faze him at all. Although he couldn't tell us himself, we are pretty sure he loved every minute of it. I believe he even upstaged the football club's own mascot. But if he did, the mascot didn't show that he was put out in any way. Naturally, there were a lot of confused and surprised faces at seeing a duck at their beloved game. But the fans seemed to love it too, as some of them still remind Barrie of it today. They were thankful that Star was there as at least it gave them something to smile about. Especially since they unfortunately lost the game! The Hospice was also really pleased as they raised over £700 that day.

Chapter Nineteen

Barrie and Star were now really developing their double act. It had occurred to Barrie that as a kid, he was really good at speaking Donald Duck. So he tried it out on Star. To his amazement, Star totally reacted to this. So this now became part of the act. Barrie would talk to Star in his own language. Barrie would happily explain to people that he taught him English whilst Star taught him Duck. This method of communication got to the point whereby Barrie had to speak to Star in "Duck" for him to take any notice! As with many children (and partners for that matter!), Star quite often had selective hearing. "Time to go now," or "To me Star, to me," was something he didn't want to hear. But there again, if Barrie spoke in Duck, Star would eventually respond.

There were some things that Star acknowledged in English though. Barrie regularly had to call Star off from chasing dogs down the street. If any got too close, Star would bop them on the nose with his beak and chase them off. Barrie would hear himself saying

"That'll do, duck. That'll do." I have to admit that I still chuckle when I see and hear this, remembering one of the final lines said from the film *Babe*: "That'll do, pig. That'll do" after the pig had successfully rounded up the sheep and led them into the pen.

In addition, Star started to acknowledge when money went into the bucket, to the point where he would take the money out of people's hands and put it in the bucket with his beak. Word started to spread and Barrie would have people asking if this was the "singing duck" they had heard about. Not quite! The two of them conversed together, but Star didn't sing. He didn't dance either, despite his performance to the camera as a duckling. The truth is, he didn't really do any tricks, apart from helping to put money in the bucket. This is why we had never entered "Britain's Got Talent" or any other talent shows. As he doesn't actually do anything other than be himself, which in itself is not usual Runner Duck behaviour. Although it was always suggested that he trained Star to do tricks, Barrie would never entertain the idea of turning him into a performing freak. Contrary to the belief of many who met them, Barrie had not trained Star to do anything. Star was who he was. And we, along with everyone else, loved him for it.

On the surface things were still okay. To the outside world, Barrie was loved by many. With his side-kick Star, he had so many supporters. By this point I had started up a Facebook page, in case we hit the limit of the number of friends allowed on the profile. I had also found another Facebook page that had sprung up: Star the Duck. Even now, I am not sure who the originator was of this, but it was, and still is, an active site.

Behind the scenes, things were not good at all.

We had received notification that we were being given three months notice on the cottage as the landlord wanted to move a family member in. I was gutted. I know we had problems with one of the neighbours and that ultimately Barrie had not felt comfortable living there for a while, but for me, I loved Hayman's Farm, my haven. I was absolutely devastated. What were we going to do? Where were we going to go? Could we take all our animals with us?

At the same time we were having trouble with our dogs. Genghis and Drake were brothers and with the arrival of Star their sibling rivalry was getting a little out of hand. They had started fighting on and off, but it was becoming more and more frequent. Barrie was already nearly at breaking point, and I was now on the verge, too.

Unfortunately, work was of no comfort either. The charity was in financial problems again so everything was looking uncertain there as well. With the possibility of me being made redundant again, this definitely didn't help when considering our options of where to move to next.

We had no alternative but to face things head on, one step at a time.

With very heavy hearts, we went to the local Dogs Trust to talk about getting Genghis re-homed. We were both tearful when filling out the forms and had prepared ourselves to hand him over. They couldn't accommodate him at that moment due to building works going on there, so we brought him home again. We knew he would need to go to a new home as it was not fair on anyone. No one was happy with the current situation. He was such a lovely creature, but wouldn't accept Drake as top dog. So they both went out of character and would fight each other. It was horrible to see. It all added extra stress to us and them. In addition to that, both Barrie and I had nightmares that Star might get caught up in the middle of one of their fights and ultimately would come off worse than either of the dogs.

At the same time we had to think about Hayman's Farm. Realistically, were we likely to find anywhere we could take all the animals with us? Both Barrie and I knew that this was highly unlikely and set about trying to find new homes for them. The last thing we wanted was to have to take them to market where they could end up on a dinner plate or at the very least, all separated and sent off in different directions.

And then there was the question of where we would live. We looked at a couple of places, but nothing had jumped out at us as being the right one. None of them up until that point, accommodated any of the animals, and didn't even guarantee that they would except a duck. There was no way we could go without Star.

It was while we were at a Country Fayre with Star that I came across another charity that re-homed dogs. After getting in touch, the very next day I was informed we had a possible new home for Genghis and a meeting was arranged to meet this potential new owner. Although I was very sad as we totally adored Genghis, it was lovely to see this other person getting along with him. It made me realise that although Genghis loved us too, and hadn't known any different as we brought him into the world as part of Meggie's second litter two years previously, he was unhappy with the current situation. He didn't like fighting either. He needed to be in a home where he was the top dog and given all the attention, not playing second fiddle to another dog and a duck. On the recommendation of the charity, I left him with his new owner for a trial period.

On returning home, although there was sadness, the dynamics with Drake and Meggie had already eased and we have to confess, none of us missed the fighting. We later found out that after a couple of weeks, Genghis was again re-homed with a new family and can only hope he is now settled and happy.

With all this uncertainty, Barrie brought up a subject I had managed to avoid for literally years: to live in a mobile home. I had absolutely and totally dissed the idea from the beginning, and even more so since I had worked my way up into management. My view was that I didn't work hard to come home to a mobile home. Barrie's view hadn't changed: it was a simpler way of life and we could potentially remain in the countryside. I still resisted the idea, but at the same time, I felt I was being backed into a corner. With work looking so uncertain, was it wise to pay loads of money to move to a place that we maybe wouldn't be able to afford later? And also not be able to take our animals to anyway? So eventually I relented and let him look into it.

There was no getting away from the fact though, that the majority of our animals would need to be re-homed: even if it was only temporary, whereby we could somehow come and collect them again at a later date. The idea of taking them to market though, was becoming more and more of a possibility with every day that passed.

That was until I happened to mention it to a friend of ours – Pippa, who said she knew someone who was looking at getting some geese. Following further discussions it seemed they were also open to the idea of taking on all of our other animals. They had several acres of land, already had some chickens and a couple of pigs, and were totally excited about the prospect of adding some geese and Runner Ducks to the mix. What a huge relief. All of the animals on Hayman's Farm were to be re-homed together, to a place where they would be loved and with lots more land than we had.

With the help of Drake we managed to get most of them together and into various crates, except for a couple of chickens who hid in the bushes. We had absolutely no chance of getting them out so we had to wait until the following day to catch them unawares. The new owners even took all the cages and little houses we had accrued over the last few years. By the time they left, Hayman's Farm was now just a boring bit of land with no life. My little haven was gone. I no longer wanted to live there anymore.

Chapter Twenty

While all this was going on, Barrie was still very much out and about with Star. There were extremely few people in the area who didn't know about or hadn't seen them. Whether or not they put money in the bucket, they would all say hello to Star as they passed. Those who hadn't heard of Star before would look on in disbelief at seeing a duck – or was it a goose - with a bow tie strolling down the street. And were even more amazed when no one else seemed to think this was in any way strange.

But this was, in all honesty, the only thing keeping Barrie sane with all the stress at home.

The 2012 London Olympics was due to start soon and the Olympic Torch was doing a nationwide tour/relay. It was due to come through North Devon, passing through several different towns and villages. Although Barrie truthfully thought this was all just hype, and in actual fact didn't really like crowds, he thought he would go along to Barnstaple to make the most of the people being there, hoping he could raise more money for the Children's Hospice.

On the outskirts of town the traffic had stopped and was being diverted, as this was the route the main procession would be taking. Even though he was in a nondescript white Astra – unfortunately we had to get rid of the 4x4, which we had lovingly hand-painted in camouflage when we first bought it – some of the kids lining the road spotted Star in the front seat. And before he knew it, they were surrounded. Somehow Barrie managed to manoeuvre the car forward, even though some of the kids had tried to get onto the bonnet, and reached the stewards. For reasons he still doesn't know, the stewards let their car go through and didn't turn them away. Barrie found himself driving down the hill where loads of people were standing on the pavement waiting for the torch procession to come through. They were cheering and clapping when they realised it was Barrie and Star in the car. They absolutely loved the attention but Barrie felt a wee bit embarrassed that they weren't in a better car. He was also waiting for the police or stewards to come and stop him at any point, realising their mistake for letting him through.

When he got to the bottom of the hill, the stewards made room for them to drive through the crowds to get to the nearby car park. Having parked the car, Barrie picked Star up and walked back, wondering as he went as to how he was going to get Star though all the people. All he had planned to do was get to the main square where they could go about their busking.

On seeing them, the stewards lifted the rope and let them both through. Barrie being a little bit slow on the uptake – as he will tell you, "I might be thick but I'm awfully slow," thought maybe they were just going to guide them through the crowds. But no. He found himself and Star, who was now waddling just in front of him, heading down the centre of the road into the heart of the town with the crowds either side. When the crowds spotted them, the shouts and screams became deafening. You see, there had been the official organisers of the Olympic Torch who had gone on ahead of the actual float and torch runner. They had warmed the crowd up and got them all excited. But the torch bearer hadn't arrived yet and all these people were hyped up. So seeing Star and Barrie – their local celebrities, coming down the street was a real treat. They had no idea that this hadn't been planned. Barrie couldn't have planned this, even if he'd tried. Meanwhile, although enjoying all the attention and being blown away by the screams and shouts, Barrie was expecting any minute for someone to come and ask them to leave.

He knew it couldn't last. He could see out of his peripheral vision two motorbike cops coming up on either side. Waiting for the inevitable arrest, he couldn't put it off any longer and looked at one of them. To his sheer amazement and relief they were smiling. In fact they were grinning. One of them gave him a salute and handed him some money for the bucket! Totally unbelievable. Not only that, the police stayed with them to the point that Star now had police outriders as escorts!

They came up to some school children. You could tell they were just bursting with excitement. The build up to the torch had been going on for weeks, but before that happened, here they were seeing Star. The screams were overpowering.

Although enjoying it and still not believing what was happening, Barrie was concerned as he couldn't hear himself think, let alone be able to communicate with Star. Thankfully though, Star was taking it all in and just waddling along, seemingly enjoying the attention as much as Barrie was.

But then some burly security men came up behind them and said they needed to move the duck out of the road immediately. Barrie calmly said that this was fine; he would pick Star up. But the security guys had a different idea and they, in their impatience to get them out of the way, started to go towards Star. Barrie tried to explain to them that they would never catch him like that, as he was a *runner* duck after all! And true to form, Star was having none of it. Before you knew it, the screams went into laughter as everyone watched these two very well-built men get increasingly frustrated and annoyed as they ran around in circles trying to pick him up. Barrie eventually caught Star, but not before the whole of the torch procession had been brought to a standstill. The torch bearer had been given no option but to wait for Star to leave before being able to continue.

Needless to say their unplanned celebrity walk of fame had been a resounding success. Barrie was told later by those who were in the surrounding offices, that they had to close the windows when Star walked past due to the noise. Some went on to say that even the windows rattled. And then they were able to open them again as the torch went by. It seemed that for some people, seeing Star was more exciting than seeing the torch bearer pass. And the school teachers who had taken their class there, found themselves struggling. The following day when asked to draw a picture of what they had seen, most of the children drew a duck and not the Olympic torch!

It was not long after this we were offered another car. It was a blue Laguna that had been painted bright yellow and decorated as a rally car. The owners had taken it over to Spain as part of the Barcelona Bangers, raising money for the Children's Hospice. They were so taken with Star, they had gone the extra mile and put a load of ducks on the roof, too. Once they had returned from the rally, they had no use for it so on a handshake Barrie swapped his Astra for the new "duckmobile". With the ducks already on the roof, there was now no doubt when Barrie and Star were in town.

Chapter Twenty-One

With all the animals gone, I no longer cared where we lived. I found myself talking more and more with Barrie about living in a mobile home. We started really looking into this to see what we could do; well aware the clock was ticking for when we needed to move out of the cottage. Even though I was totally stressed out and gutted, I couldn't help also being a little bit excited at the prospect of change. A new chapter was beginning.

Through a friend, we heard about a mobile home for sale so we went to have a look. My heart sank when I first saw it. A tired old mobile home that certainly wasn't pretty like our cottage. But I begrudgingly was also pleasantly surprised. It was relatively big, similar to a flat really. It was quite far inland so not close to the sea like our other Devon homes had been. But that said, it was surrounded by the most amazing countryside with fantastic views. It hadn't been lived in for a very long time so was absolutely filthy and full of cobwebs, wasn't connected to any utilities, and was sitting on land that was connected to a mechanics yard.

With Barrie in charge, I soon realised they were shaking hands. We would be renting this on site having been hooked up to electric, gas, and water. Job done. The owner of the mobile home seemed to be happy to accommodate our reduced family - myself, Barrie, two dogs and a duck.

Part of me was excited. The other part: desperately sad.

With just a few weeks to go before we needed to be out of the cottage, we started to go through all of the stuff we had accumulated over the years. We had to arrange for all of our furniture to go. And because we would be downsizing in a big way from a 3-bedroomed cottage to a small 2-bedroomed mobile home with no storage, we had to get rid of pretty much anything that wasn't sentimental. I had booked the last week of August off work so I could focus on getting this all done properly.

However, it didn't get that far. The previous week at work I had got the distinct impression that something big was going down. As I was no longer part of the senior management team following my role change the previous year, I was therefore no longer privy to what was happening. I found out with everyone else later that week; another charity was taking our charity over, and they were only taking fifteen of the current staff. The rest of us were being made redundant there and then. We all sat there in disbelief. Many people were in tears with their first thought being how they were going to pay the rent or mortgage. It was nearly the end of the month and none of us would get paid. I had to hand in my laptop and phone and leave with immediate effect.

For me it was a shock, but not a massive surprise. And in complete honesty I was also quite relieved. Although the five years I had been there had been really good for my personal development, and most of the time I had really enjoyed it, over the past few months I really hadn't found any fulfilment. It had been a complete and utter stress, and I had actually found it quite difficult.

I was pleased to have the time to focus on the move. It really was now a complete new beginning: a fresh start in every way.

A week later and the furniture had all been sold to an auction house. Lots of our other bits and pieces had either been chucked out, given away to friends, or given to charity. We were sleeping on the floor with our possessions in boxes and bags around us ready to move. The dogs, being intuitive, knew something was happening and were very uneasy about the whole thing and probably as stressed as we were. Star on the other hand, didn't seem that bothered. As long as he was near his dad, he was happy. Besides, his bedroom was still in situ at the time so he was all right. Even if the rest of us weren't!

And things weren't straightforward either: the mobile home had only just been moved into its new position and it hadn't been hooked up to electricity yet, but time had run out. We had to move in anyway.

With a couple of my friends, Kim and Hilary, who were now ex-work colleagues and therefore jobless too, we set about trying to give the mobile home a good clean. Years' worth of cobwebs and dirt were everywhere, but with some hard graft and trading on the goodwill of the mechanic nearby for hot water, we were all really pleased, and pleasantly surprised. The interior actually came up okay. With the curtains up and some of the little trinkets and pictures I had insisted on keeping, it started to feel like it was some sort of home. While all this was going on, Star stayed with Barrie to supervise the cleaning that he was doing at the cottage. Drake and Meggie stayed in the car. Barrie worked on cleaning the cottage for several days with the grateful help of our next door neighbour, and eventually closed the cottage up. He never wanted to set foot in that place again.

By the time he arrived at the mobile home it was looking in good shape and quite homey. We still didn't have electricity or running water. Thankfully it was the beginning of September so it didn't get dark too early and wasn't too cold. Luckily I had saved the candles from being given away so at least we had some light.

Following our first night in the mobile home, now affectionately called The Manor, Barrie got up bright and early with a spring in his step. For the first time in months and months, he did not have a panic attack. He was truly happy as he had wanted this for so long. That in itself was enough to bring down some of the stress levels that I had felt over the past few months. Star also seemed very happy with this new home having found a very cosy space to put his bedroom. The dogs absolutely loved their new playground: a huge gravelled yard that was shut off from everyone by a large metal gate, which was kept closed most of the time. They just loved checking it all out, including an old steam roller that was rusting away in the corner.

There were still many things to sort out and lots to do. So I was swept up in getting the place organised and didn't really have time to worry about the future. As the days and weeks passed, Barrie and I also became so much closer. It sounds silly, but we became friends again. I somehow started to de-stress and enjoy simpler living. Electricity had eventually been connected after a couple of days, although this was limited to 13 amps and therefore we had to be very careful not to have certain things on at the same time without blowing a fuse. For example, if we had the kettle on we couldn't have the toaster too. I managed to have a TV installed, which I was more pleased about than Barrie. I felt this was very important to me: my way of switching off. But that said, we started to spend more quality time with each other: playing cards and Monopoly... something neither of us had done in years. Certainly not in the many years we had been together. Star would also join in with the game, usually being annoying to be honest: moving the pieces or cards around and quite often disrupting the game.

Although promised, neither the water nor the gas were connected. So we made do with a small electric heater, bottled water, and also water from the hose outside. Barrie came into his own here: he got a really good system going to make life easier. He also taught me the real basics of a strip wash. But oh how I missed a bath or a shower!

Despite having no job and living very basically, things were actually okay.

Chapter Twenty-Two

By now the amount Barrie and Star had actually raised was literally thousands of pounds for the Children's Hospice from their bucket collections. Their best day was nearly £400 in just a matter of hours. This was due to a good mix of fantastic weather, school holidays, living in a tourist area where the number of people in the area pretty much doubled, and the fact that Star was still somewhat of a novelty to most people. However, their work wasn't finished yet. Not by a long shot.

Things were coming to a head. It seems three councils had come together and had contacted the Children's Hospice asking for a meeting to "resolve the matter of Barrie and Star". They invited themselves to Little Bridge House for this meeting. As the main topic of discussion Barrie naturally wanted to be present. And as I was no longer working I was available to be there too. The Hospice informed us that the councils hadn't invited us. It seems they wanted to talk about us and not to us. That was *so* not going to happen. Luckily we didn't have to gatecrash the meeting, as the Hospice agreed with us.

We were the first to arrive at the small meeting room and sat down at the table looking at the Remembrance Tree, which was set off to the side: a tree that had messages pinned to the branches dedicated to those children who had passed over. You couldn't help but reflect and have a quiet moment.

Eventually we were joined by a member of the Hospice staff and two others representing two of the Councils. It seems one of the Councils couldn't make it, or possibly had second thoughts?

Barrie put his hand out to shake hands of one of them, smiled, and said,

"You look familiar. Have we met somewhere before?" At which she curtly responded,

"No, I can assure you we definitely have not."

Barrie is very good at remembering faces so there is every possibility he might have seen her before. Whether this was the case or not, I was more than a little taken aback by her tone. They immediately started by mentioning an Act of Parliament dating back to 1916. They had even brought a copy of it with them along with a pile of other documents they wanted to bombard the Children's Hospice with. They clearly pointed out that Barrie was breaking the law by not applying for this licence and therefore was not playing by the rules of this Act. All the time they spoke as if neither Barrie nor I were in the room, and so addressed Barrie as a third party. Despite being blatantly ignored, Barrie pointed out that this was no longer 1916 and the world was a very different place. He also went on to explain that there was rarely any other charities out on the street, that they were indeed buskers, and what about tourism? He gave a really good case. Of course he understood that rules were rules, but couldn't they just make an exception to these rules in acknowledgement for what they brought to the high street? Surely there was a compromise to be made here.

They continued to look at and address the Hospice representative and continued to state their case that Barrie and Star were indeed breaking the law. Barrie asked what would happen if he took out his own bucket? Therefore he would appear to be collecting for himself, but would in fact still be donating all the funds to the Children's Hospice. To that suggestion the lady replied, again looking directly at the Hospice representative,

"If you do that I will be very disappointed. Very disappointed indeed."

Barrie had heard enough. Here he was sitting next to a Remembrance Tree in the Children's Hospice being told absolutely and categorically that they would not even entertain the idea of bending the rules even by a little bit for this wonderful charity. He felt sick so he got up and left. Just walked out.

I sat there stunned and not quite knowing what to do next. Should I walk out too, showing my disgust? No, I couldn't do that. I am a different breed to Barrie, and although I couldn't believe the way the meeting was going, I found myself sitting there until the end, which was not long after. I felt sorry for the Hospice. They couldn't control what Barrie did. He was not a paid member of staff. He was someone who happened to donate what he collected to their charity, not forgetting the other good work carried out when he and Star visited the children. They no doubt felt themselves completely backed into a corner. They had often told Barrie how pleased they were with what he and Star did. The money they had collected so far and the profile of the Children's Hospice being raised as well over the past year since Star had been associated with them.

I sat across from the two council representatives who appeared very smug and happy with themselves. They pushed over the application form to me, smiling, and actually looking at me and therefore acknowledging my presence for the first time. They informed me that if Barrie and Star continued to go out collecting without completing the form, we would find ourselves in court.

The councils were sticking religiously to this particular Act: The "Police, Factories, etc (Miscellaneous Provisions) Act 1916". So what was going on in 1916 to bring about a law surrounding charity collections on the street?

1916 was right in the middle of World War One; with the Boer War having taken place only a couple of decades previously. Those who were injured or maimed in either of those wars came home and had no alternative but to either beg on the streets or enter the workhouse, or poorhouse as it was also known. Neither of these options were desirable, but as there was no welfare scheme or pension to support them they found they had little choice. Many did whatever they could to avoid either scenario. Some of the lucky ones had some meagre savings and managed to purchase things like matches, cigarettes, and similar at wholesale prices and sell them on the street at a reduced rate to the shops. It was also around this time where a social conscience was starting to grow. Open soup kitchens started to spring up and other small enterprises being the start of the early charities, all popping up alongside the beggars and pedlars. Many of the smaller towns didn't have a pavement and the road itself was little more than what we would consider a dirt track today. The early model car was still only in its infancy, so only really owned by the upper-class, and therefore transport was predominantly still beast driven – usually horses, but sometimes cattle, too. With the side of the road overrun, the local people - including the gentry - were forced to walk towards the middle of the road, or quagmire as they so regularly became. Quite often it would not have been pleasant to walk in. Forgetting the smell, the fashion for ladies were long dresses. And wellington boots certainly hadn't been invented at this stage.

Councils existed at this time, but they were unpaid workers. The police authorities had the greater power. The townsfolk put pressure on these authorities to take action to bring some control to the situation, where people could go into the growing main streets without feeling overwhelmed by so many people, including the newly emerged charities asking for money.

And now this same Act, almost one hundred years later, was being used against Barrie and Star. At the meeting it was only this one Act that was presented. No mention being made of The Charities Act 1960, 1992 and 2006 or the Charitable Collections (Transitional Provisions) Order 1974. Having looked into this more closely later, we realised that it also stated within the 1916 Act that the powers were "discretionary." As the councils at the meeting chose to refer only to this one particular Act, then surely they could have used their discretion and chosen to be more flexible and at least be open to compromise?

In a sense you could completely understand why this licence might be necessary. Nobody wants the streets to be inundated with people collecting for charity. But the fact of the matter is there were not many charities out on the streets very often anyway. Quite regularly Barrie and Star found they were the only ones there on any one day. Occasionally they were joined by a fellow busker or a Big Issue seller. Even on the days when the charities decided to go out collecting, it was very rarely on the main streets they chose. And when they did, it would be maybe one or two people holding a collection tin. Their preferred location was usually on the entrance to an out of town supermarket. Many of the charities seem to have pretty much abandoned the high streets.

The meeting had finished and I found Barrie seething outside. He was furious, especially as we watched the two council representatives both leaving looking very happy. Yes, rules are rules, but surely there were exceptions and a compromise somewhere? But no. To us it appeared that they were clearly closed off to any suggestions. They certainly weren't taking into account what the public wanted.

So what if he was to ask the public? He had many an ear after all. What would they have to say about this? Barrie decided to get on his soap box – literally...

Chapter Twenty-Three

Barrie found an old wooden box. Took it to the high streets and literally stood on it, telling the general public what the councils were doing to try to get him and Star off the streets. I happened to be in town on one of those days, and saw him on this little box with Star standing tall next to him. My heart was in my mouth. It was such a brave thing to do and I have to admit I was scared stiff for him. He really was now putting his head above the parapet. Of course he had been doing this from the first moment he walked out onto the high street with Star in the beginning, but surely this was taking it to the extreme? How would people take to this? I know he had a lot of support, but this was a little bit weird. He didn't see me watching as I was a little distance away, but I watched as he talked to a small crowd. There were several who walked straight past, not batting an eyelid. Others who went past laughed or gave him a funny look. My heart went out to him. Barrie was such a stubborn old thing. Ever since he was a small kid, he never backed down from a fight. And that is how he saw it: a fight against the councils who were trying to stop him do something that was not only raising money and awareness for a very good cause, but also the tourism and entertainment being brought into the town centres. Forgetting those who took no notice, there were plenty more who did listen and did care.

The councils now found themselves literally inundated with letters, emails, and phone calls showing their support for their two favourite celebrities.

A year on from when they first hit the headlines, Barrie and Star found themselves in the local paper and on local TV again, but it wasn't a good news story this time. The media agreed with us – so why didn't the councils?

Meanwhile, Barrie continued to go out with Star onto the streets armed with a bucket, his own bucket without the Children's Hospice logo on. And the money collected was donated to the Hospice despite what the councils had said.

September was Carnival Season. The Children's Hospice had a float in the Barnstaple carnival. They asked if Star would be part of this. Although we had lived in Devon for nearly ten years we hadn't actually been to any of the carnivals so the whole thing was completely new to us. We had no idea what to expect.

The Hospice had managed to get a bus donated for the day and the children, volunteers, and staff had decorated it with a Narnia theme. The staff and volunteers were all dressed up in the same theme. Barrie and I looked a bit boring in comparison with just our Children's Hospice T-shirts on. Star was wearing one of his more colourful bow ties though.

Barrie, Star and I were to walk in front of the bus. Being novices to the whole experience we had gone down to the starting point with the rest of the group in the bus, not realising that the actual carnival didn't start for a good couple of hours. So we found ourselves hanging around. Neither Barrie nor Star are any good at waiting. I babysat them both at the back of the bus, trying to keep Star quiet and low key until it was time for the event to start.

There were so many other floats there from all sorts of different organisations and schools. All were brightly decorated and many of them played very loud music. I was concerned that Star would be daunted by this. But as Barrie pointed out, if he hadn't been fazed by the shouts and screams at the torch relay or the noise of the fans at the football match, then this should be fine.

It was time. I walked alongside Barrie with Star slightly ahead of us. The other Hospice collectors were very nearby with the bus following. It seemed that the annual carnival was a big event here in Barnstaple and the streets were filled with both adults and children alike. They all clutched the small change they had collected over time specifically to put into the buckets and collection tins of their favourite floats.

In spite of the loud music and activity all around, Star appeared very at ease with his surroundings. I was feeling a little uncomfortable being out on show like this, but also very proud: watching Star and Barrie stopping and interacting with the crowd. Star had, by this point, developed a particular mannerism: Barrie would introduce Star to whoever and Star in turn would bob his head, saying hello. To see it time and time again was amazing. Neither of them seemed to tire of this. The bus soon overtook us and we found ourselves walking just slightly ahead of a tractor pulling another float. I was a little anxious having these huge wheels that were nearly as tall as me literally a metre or so behind, but I was the only one to be nervous of this. Star and Barrie continued to walk around and stop whenever they were called over. So the tractor had to stop, too. In addition to this we found ourselves right in the middle of a group who were on roller blades. They sped past at great speed doing all sorts of tricks along the way. I was starting to panic a little, but not Barrie and Star. I was out of my comfort zone, but then I was in the alien world of Barrie and Star and this was bread and butter to them.

By the time we had made our way around the circuit everyone was on a high, but also very tired. With the long wait and anticipation prior to it starting, and then the actual walk albeit very slowly, we were ready to head home and also for something to eat, so we headed for a drive-through. Many of the others who had either taken part or had been spectators all had the same idea and we found ourselves in a queue. We didn't go unnoticed.

Firstly, we were in the duckmobile and therefore sitting in a bright yellow car with ducks on the roof. Secondly, Star liked to look out of the window with Drake by his side. The people were happily looking back at Star as the car made slow progress towards the front. And as regularly happened, the staff were pretty freaked out to see the duck staring at them as they handed over the Big Mac and fries!

This wasn't the only carnival. We were also invited along to the Carnival in the small market town of South Molton a few weeks later. Only this time, without the Children's Hospice float. As before, there were absolutely loads of floats, many playing loud music. Having learned from last time we arrived a lot nearer the time it was due to start. On a whim, I also entered Star into a competition for the best outfit. However, as the competition got under way, the organisers weren't sure which class to put Star into. Whichever one they finally went with, Star won first prize. I was a very proud Mum, especially because he was wearing a new bow tie for the occasion.

When the carnival eventually set off we just tagged along, as we were not part of any particular float. Marching ahead of us, Star soon caught up with the local pipe band. And that is where he stayed. Even Barrie couldn't tempt him away. He seemed to be lulled by the pipes and even waddled in time to the beat of the drums. Credit to the band, they all managed to keep their cool and kept playing even though they were all aware they now had a new member who at times was walking right in the middle of them. Having decided he wanted to join this group, it was Star who determined when he wanted a change of scene and left them. I think it was down to his impatience, as the whole flotilla had stopped due to a huge bend in the road and had to take it slowly, that Star dictated that we move on. We found ourselves on the street all alone, being called left, right, and centre by the crowd. Again out of my comfort zone, I didn't know which way to go, who to go up to. There were no barriers so many came up to us and put money in the bucket. As always, Barrie and Star totally did their own thing and gave their attention to as many people as they could.

Then disaster struck. I watched it happen. Star had gone to the side of the road and decided he was hungry so picked up and ate a discarded chip. Obviously it hadn't gone down properly, and I could see him struggling, shaking his head from side to side, and looking like he might be in trouble. We were luckily near the end of the circuit and when Barrie eventually understood what I was trying to say and saw that Star was struggling he picked him up - a sign in itself that he was feeling poorly as he didn't try to run away. We rushed to the vets, which was not only conveniently close by, but also open due to the fact they were giving out tea, coffee, and biscuits to those taking part in the carnival. Barrie took him inside following one of the vets. They were gone for a while and I was worried but so, so thankful the vets were there and open. Not that they were expecting to serve anything other than tea that evening. They finally came out. After some nifty work from the vet, the chip had been dislodged and Star had drunk loads of water. No harm done.

Again for us, the carnival had been a great success.

Chapter Twenty-Four

The weeks and months that followed was a very strange time for me. Realisation had set in that not only was I unemployed, but I was also living in a mobile home. Despite the limited electricity and still no running water, I was actually okay and managing to adjust, albeit at a much slower rate than Barrie, Star and the dogs, but getting by nonetheless. I think it helped that Barrie had brought in all his training from the Army and Navy, along with his general survival instincts. We had a really good system getting the water in, and other little tricks that he came up with to make life that little bit easier, something I would never have managed or even contemplated had I been on my own. Also it was totally obvious that Barrie was happy, even with the existing problems with the councils. His panic attacks and shaking – which at its peak was literally from head to toe and quite worrying at times – had subsided. And we were spending lots of quality time together. Dominoes had now joined the array of games that we happily played together. Star loved his little game with this, too: knocking them over or even picking them up in his beak. Both of us were re-learning the art of relaxation: something we realised we hadn't done for a very long time.

We now also had a new family of animals - the wild birds. We had managed to rig up a bespoke bird table in the form of our old stepladder. A washing line went across from the ladder to a tree with all manner of goodies attached. It paid off. Armed with our bird-watching books we saw all kinds of different species come to our little restaurant: Robins, Chaffinches, several different species of Tit, the Great Spotted Woodpecker, and even a Jay and his family.

Since moving, Barrie and Star went more and more frequently to South Molton. They had a pannier market every Thursday and Saturday. Unlike the other councils, it seemed that this particular council had welcomed them with open arms. From the very first visit they appeared to realise that they were a real hit with both the stallholders and the visitors/buyers alike, which in turn drew more people to the market. They even went so far as to provide free parking for the duckmobile. Star loved going there too, not only to meet some of his favourite locals – from babies to the retired – but also to see one of his favourite stall holders – Dan the Fish Man. Star always knew he could rely on Dan to give him some food. We usually discourage people from feeding Star as we don't want him to come to expect it. It also means we can control what he is eating and when. That said, this was different. He fed him no ordinary food: scallops no less. Star was a diva duck as we know, so only the best for him. Having said that, he would happily accept cheese, tomato, and prawns from his Mum at any opportunity, usually standing on my foot so I had no choice but to feed him one of his favourites every time I entered the kitchen!

This little town was now the only place where Barrie took the Children's Hospice bucket due to the town council being so happy and accommodating with them. The weird thing was, had they been granted the licence, they wouldn't have been allowed to collect in the pannier markets as they are deemed private property. So in actual fact, by Barrie staying in the pannier market he was totally acting within the 1916 law.

One of Star's regulars was a lovely old lass, possibility in her eighties. Always really well dressed, colour coordinated, quietly well-spoken and she always put money in the bucket. On one of her visits she asked Barrie if they were still having trouble with the councils. He confirmed that they were. She said she was there to help them. He wondered at that point whether she sat on the council, or knew someone who did or whatever. She explained that you had to talk to them in a language they would understand. Barrie said he had done everything he could.

With that she said, "Well, have you thought about telling them to **** off?"

This was the very last thing Barrie expected her to say, based on the way she had always conducted herself in the past. Not to mention her age; part of a generation who very rarely swore, but he and others who were gathered around, couldn't help but laugh as this appeared so out of character. On a serious note though, it just proved the strength of feeling their supporters had.

Even with all the relaxing and quality time with each other, I was feeling very uneasy. For a little while I was enjoying the down time, the space, and the new surroundings. But now I was very aware that I wasn't doing anything or going anywhere. For Barrie and Star nothing had really changed except for the location: just further to travel. They still continued to go out fairly regularly doing what they did - entertaining the crowds, and busking. For me though, I was starting to get a bit disheartened. It didn't help that I had no idea what I should be doing next, what my next career move should be. I couldn't be pigeon-holed, which had its advantages, but also had some major disadvantages. If I didn't really know what I should be doing and which direction to take then how would recruitment agencies and employers know?

Christmas was looming with not much redundancy money left and not knowing what the future held. When I had lost my job, I was relieved that the roller coaster had stopped. Now I wanted to get back on again, but didn't know how. It seemed to me that Barrie and Star were on a gentle roller coaster, merrily coasting along with the occasional small loop the loop of intrigue, excitement and sometimes unpleasantness from those who didn't want to see them out and about. Me, I was falling into a black hole, feeling insecure and not needed. I desperately yearned for a bath and, quite frankly, a life!

In addition to that, The Manor was cold. Freezing in fact. As the gas had never been connected due to the fact the mobile home was too old and the pipes were too knackered, we were relying on two little electric heaters. That obviously didn't help towards our 13-amp limit either. And given that the mobile home is made of metal, when it was cold outside, it was cold inside. Sometimes the electric went off usually due to a fuse blowing and more than once this happened during the middle of the night. It certainly wasn't a laughing matter. With two duvets, pyjamas, cardigan, hot water bottle, and bed socks, it was still freezing. Even Barrie – my trusted second hot water bottle – was feeling the cold too. And being at home all day you didn't warm up easily either. Having said that, as soon as the sun came out, it had the greenhouse effect and would soon warm up. Some days it literally went from one extreme to the other. As you can imagine, the novelty of living at The Manor was starting to wear off.

A few weeks before Christmas we received a call out of the blue. Would Barrie stand in for Father Christmas at a local Christmas Fayre as the original Santa had taken ill at the last minute? Although this call was unexpected, Barrie had been a stand-in Santa in various locations throughout the area in the previous years. Barrie took pride in the fact that he was a Santa with a difference. He refused to wear what is thought as the traditional outfit, choosing instead to wear jodhpurs, riding boots complete with spurs, with a long red coat. The only traditional parts were the white fluffy trim on the coat, red hat with trim, and the trademark white beard. He also didn't sit in a chair, but preferred to kneel down and talk to the children, changing the tone and conversation to suit the age.

He readily accepted, as long as he could bring the duck. I wasn't very convinced this was a good idea, though. I know Star hates it when he is not with Barrie. If Barrie were to leave the room and close the door behind him without letting him follow, Star would stomp up and down the room in a panic, making long, loud wailing quacks until Barrie came back. But this was in the evening so surely we could just put him to bed early? No. Barrie was not going to be Santa's stand-in without his special little helper. So off they went.

Santa sat in his grotto, and his little helper sat behind the seat on a little ledge. At first, Star wasn't all that interested in what was going on and settled down to sleep. But then every so often he would pop his head up and join in with Santa, quacking away. Both children and parents alike were taken by surprise as the duck-elf emerged, but it added to the experience and the fun of the visit. It was a long and tiring evening for both Santa and his duck-elf. Instead of the previous year of thirty minutes of visiting, it had gone on for over two hours with queues continually stretched out the door. Take note Father Christmas - Indian Runner Ducks make very good elves!

One thing that touched me during those dark days was the Children's Hospice Carol Service. We felt very privileged to be invited. Those children who were well enough were in attendance alongside their families. They had a donkey that came in at the beginning, which didn't take too kindly to Star getting in his way and possibly even upstaging him on his grand annual appearance. Not that Star was bothered. And there were hand-bell ringers too. Star manoeuvred himself so he was right in the middle of the congregation. Watching him, Barrie realised Star really enjoyed the singing so he knelt down next to him and started quacking away. If I could understand Duck speak, I am sure Star would tell me that We Three Kings was his favourite Christmas Carol: Star of wonder, Star of light, Star with royal beauty bright. I think Star being there added just that little bit of an extra something to an event that in itself was very, very moving. We felt a little subdued but content on the journey home. The lovely service really put things into perspective. I realised that although I was feeling very low in myself, I actually had an awful lot to be grateful for.

Chapter Twenty-Five

January felt like a very, very long month for me. I had attended a couple of interviews in the last few months, but there was nothing on the horizon. I was feeling lost.

Back in November we had been contacted by Real People magazine. The Children's Hospice had entered Star into a competition for the Community Pet of the Year Award. For our part, it involved having a telephone interview with them so they could write an article. What they produced was great and the magazine staff were really excited with Star's story. We now had to wait with bated breath as to whether we had won or not. It was towards the end of January that we heard Star hadn't won. Although we didn't necessarily expect to win, it was just another knock back at a time when we were already both on a low ebb.

In addition to that, it had been a really bad winter for the rain, even worse than the previous year. There was flooding everywhere. We didn't have any literally on our doorstep, like other poor souls not too far from us, but we did have continual flooding just down the road and regularly found we couldn't get out without a near-on ten-mile detour.

Barrie absolutely loved hearing the rain on the roof. He found it soothing and comforting. I understood where he was coming from, but didn't quite feel the same.

And the wind. Wow, the whole place rocked! Many a time I was more than a little freaked out, but Barrie just loved it and kept telling me not to worry. I must admit, I have no idea what Star and the dogs thought of the noise and rocking. I reckon it was probably only me who was actually affected by it and wonder whether the animals were even bothered!

One silver lining to that month was an article that came out in the Devon Life magazine. A freelance writer had spotted Barrie and Star out and about and had asked if she could do an article on them. She had actually interviewed and written this back in the summer before we moved. And now it had finally come out: a three-page spread. Fantastic write up with some great photos. Although it brought back some melancholy memories of times past at the cottage with all the animals, we had brilliant feedback from all those who read it. We sent a copy out to Nicola, Barrie's daughter in Australia, who also really loved it. She also loved all the posh houses and great estates that were advertised in there and it started her dreaming about winning the lottery so she and Ethan could come over here and buy one of those places for us all to live in. You and me both Nicky Nu!

It wasn't only me who was feeling a little unhappy. Meggie, our Kelpie-

Collie was also struggling at times. Being of older years she could get a little grumpy. And she didn't take kindly to Star bossing her and Drake around. Barrie had already started to relegate her to the boot of the car and not on the seat with Drake and Star as she had a tendency to chew Star's man tail. It had taken Barrie a while to work out why Star's sign of drake-hood was missing! Since being at The Manor, Meggie was starting to get more and more annoyed with Star's habit of snapping and poking at her and Drake. Star didn't do it to hurt them or be in any way malicious. I think it was more that he just felt superior to them and was being cheeky. But Meggie had had enough and lost her rag one day and snapped back. Of course dogs have teeth, unlike ducks, and a small chunk was taken out of Star's beak. We were beside ourselves. Meggie was shocked and upset. Not only at what she had done, but also that her master was not happy with her. Again Star was taken off to the vets. They soon came back armed with painkillers and a dog muzzle. Meggie sulked for the rest of the evening in the corner with the muzzle on and Star was unusually subdued, happily accepting cuddles not just from Barrie but from me too. He even came and sat on my shoulder for a while, which was very out of character. I couldn't help but milk that moment for everything it was worth!

Although Meggie was less than impressed with Star at times, Drake was a different kettle of fish altogether.

Collies originate from the wolf, where they worked as a pack. So with Drake, his leader of the pack was Barrie. Although Drake would have seen all of our animals as potential prey, when we had Hayman's Farm, Drake could be kept off the lead with them and would continue to work and round them up all day if left alone. But he would never hurt them. He wouldn't do that as only Barrie could do that as the leader of the pack.

So how is it that Drake and Star had such a strong bond? As a Collie he would have naturally looked at Star as prey, and therefore something to round up and keep close until the leader said it is all right to kill. But as with the other animals, Barrie could leave them alone together all day and no harm would come to Star. I don't think that Drake saw Star as prey any more. I think he now saw him as a member of the family and actually a friendship had formed. I believe he also saw him as a younger brother and with that, a pain in the backside. Nevertheless, he cares for him and protects him. The interaction between them is incredible. If we had had Star first or when Drake was just a puppy then you could kind of understand it as they would have both been young and would have grown up together. Duckling and puppy like the kitten and the mouse or chick. But Drake was three years old and top dog when Star first hatched and went straight to the top of the pecking order. You hear stories of babies being attacked by the pet dog purely out of jealousy. Yes, Star may have been prey in the beginning and Drake could have been jealous of the attention given to him by the master – which was more than likely why he and Genghis started to fight - but over time they had developed a friendship and a strong bond. The only reason we put Star in a cage at night is because he is mischievous and a bit of a naughty duck and does like to stir the dogs up and annoy them. He would probably not give them much peace and try to poke them all the time. At the same time, Star does like his own space and I think his cage/bedroom is his own little haven where he has his own space.

Does Drake realise Star is special? We believe that he acknowledges that he gets more attention than him. But then Drake gets quite a lot of attention himself these days. Not just the fact that he is a striking black and white long-haired Collie with hints of brown on his eyebrows and feet, and has a lovely, friendly, laid-back nature, but many comments are made about seeing a Collie and a duck sitting on the front seat of the car together.

There was one time in the winter. It was freezing cold and Star, Barrie, and Drake (with Meggie in the very back in the boot area) were driving somewhere. As usual, Star was in the front seat. He is not happy when I come along with them as he is then relegated to the back seat and sulks by facing the corner! All of a sudden he turned around and waddled through the gap hopping onto the back seat, and snuggled up next to Drake. We could only assume he was feeling a bit chilly and wanted some warmth. Drake didn't mind at all. After all, what are big brothers for?

What does Star think of Drake? Part of me thinks he doesn't really care as he is a bit of a diva and really is Star by name and Star by nature. However, I think he also loves Drake in his own way. He likes to annoy him and wind him up, but also knows that Drake is his protector and he trusts him. He knows that if he pokes Drake in the eye, bops him on the snout, or walks up his back to get to his dad, no harm will come to him. Drake is very docile and even if he hadn't built a good friendship with Star, he still wouldn't have minded.

The bond with Star and Barrie was instant, but the bond with Star and Drake has developed, matured over time and blossomed. I don't think Drake is looking after him for his master any more. I think he now genuinely cares for him.

As for Meggie and Star: their relationship reminds us of several years ago, not long after moving to Devon, when Meggie was still quite young, on a whim we had bought a budgie. Barrie let the budgie out for the first time and it flew straight into Meggie's mouth! I screamed, Meggie spat, the bird shook, and Barrie laughed. From then on, Meggie and the budgie had an unusual relationship – safely through the bars in the cage, (certainly when I was home anyway) situated on the floor, where Meggie was transfixed whilst the budgie tweeted very loudly in her ear. Star is even bossier than the budgie ever was, but they appear to have come to an understanding.

Star has learned the hard way not to annoy Meggie. There are still a couple of hairy moments when I worry that they might clash, so to be safe Meggie has to keep her muzzle on. She can get transfixed by Star and will follow him about, but there are other times when they are both sitting quietly side by side having a nap.

Chapter Twenty-Six

With January coming to a close I was really starting to feel the pressure. My redundancy money was almost spent as we had used this to keep afloat, and the Job Seekers Allowance (JSA) alone, along with Barrie's basic pension was not enough to survive on even if we were living in a mobile home. To add to the pressure, my JSA was going to be coming to an end in one month's time. How were we going to survive? I desperately needed to get a job. Not just financially, but also for my own sanity.

I had a meeting with the job centre, which was in addition to the regular soul-destroying bi-weekly meetings I had to go to. It was to discuss why I had not yet found employment. The guy I saw, on the face of it, was pleasant enough, but what he told me just pushed me further under. Having worked in recruitment for five years, I knew how to write a Curriculum Vitae (CV). Okay, I admit it is harder to write about yourself than put one together for others. I knew the layout and what should be included where. But this guy totally ripped mine to shreds. He also told me that I should take my degree off as it was irrelevant. I was gob-smacked. It is debatable as to whether my degree had actually come in useful throughout my career, but I was very proud of it nonetheless and therefore in my eyes it definitely should remain on there. As he went on, shattering my confidence bit by bit throughout the hour and a half meeting, I realised that he was basically telling me that unless I started looking at all of the factory, warehouse and cleaning jobs within a one hundred-mile radius, then the JSA would definitely not be considered longer than the allocated six months. I really didn't want to hear any of that and I was now truly and utterly at rock bottom. I could see no way out of it.

That was on a Tuesday. By the weekend his words had finally sunk in and although I was still really annoyed with him for such a de-motivating talk, I also realised that it had given me a well and truly needed kick up the backside. I was not going to be defeated. It occurred to me that although I had dutifully checked out about a dozen job sites on the Internet each and every day, and applied for several different jobs each and every week, what I really needed to do was get myself in front of the recruitment agencies, in person. So making a list of every single job agency within a fifty-mile radius, and printing off many copies of my CV, I started making a plan in which I would visit each and every one of them. Whilst finalising this plan, a text came through from an agency asking if I was interested in a temporary job, relatively local, for two weeks. I figured this was probably a text that had been sent out on mass as I hadn't even registered with this agency as far as I was aware, but I called them back anyway. By the end of the day they confirmed I had got the job and started two days later.

It all happened so quickly I barely had time to think. The job itself was routine admin work, but I totally didn't care. It was a job. I was back in collar. Back in business. Back in the big wide world again.

Chapter Twenty-Seven

Star and Barrie continued going out with their bucket, but with me now bringing in a wage, Barrie felt a lot less guilty about collecting, as despite the fact that we were broke, the money raised from the busking still went to the charity. Having said that, they didn't get out as much as they would have liked as the weather had been horrendous.

Letters from the councils were still being received, threatening legal action if Barrie was to continue. What we couldn't understand though, was that we had been tipped off by someone within one of the councils that at least one of them was indeed backing off. They had received so many letters, emails, and phone calls from the general public berating them for pursuing Barrie and Star, not to mention the bad publicity when the story had hit the headlines a couple of months before. We were told that our story had even sparked a debate on the national current affairs show "What the Papers Say" on television. But it would seem that the councils just couldn't help themselves. We suspect that part of their continued pursuit was also pressure they received from other charities who did apply for this licence once in a blue moon, and who possibly felt that Barrie and Star were bucking the system.

The panic attacks started up again with a vengeance not long after I started back at work. I soon realised that although Barrie appeared on the whole to be very happy, and was certainly content living in the mobile home, which I still found odd, he had been putting a brave face on things, stepping up to the plate all the time I was out of work and feeling so low. Now I was feeling better within myself and money was coming back in again, he dropped his guard and his fears had returned. It seems each time he went out busking with Star, he was a nervous wreck. Would it be today that he would be arrested? Verbally or physically abused by an animal rights person, jealous busker, or charity worker?

One day when Star and Barrie were out on the high street, a policeman came up to them.

Here we go thought Barrie. *He is going to arrest me.*

What happened next really surprised him. The policeman told him that not long ago they had received a call from one of the councils asking them to arrest Barrie. The police asked what crime he had committed and their response: fraud. The police commented that fraud was a very serious offence and asked them to explain in what way Barrie had been fraudulent. It seems the council went on to say that Barrie had been seen out with a plain bucket, which he claimed was collecting for himself, but in actual fact was going to the Children's Hospice. That is fraud, they claimed. The money was not going to where he was saying it was.

Were the police really going to arrest Barrie for fraud? The whole thing was laughable and the policeman had told him such.

It might have been a laugh, but we didn't find it very funny. That the council were prepared to go this far by trying to get Barrie a criminal record. It was shocking really.

Barrie wished he had known this a few months previously when he was on his soap box. If the make-shift wooden box had not fallen apart having been left out in the heavy rain, he would have got back onto it again.

Chapter Twenty-Eight

Since moving to The Manor, Barrie had found a new pub to frequent: The Old Courthouse in Chulmleigh. They had welcomed Barrie and Star with open arms from the very beginning. Even to the point of laminating and putting up the various magazine and news articles written about them both. Star had not only charmed the locals and tourists alike in there, but also had befriended the old pub dog, Shula. As was becoming more and more apparent, Star didn't take kindly to dogs invading his space. But this old dog was not seen as a threat in any way and they were quite often seen snuggling up beside each other next to the open fire.

It was whilst at this pub one afternoon when Barrie realised something: Star wanted to be on the same level as others, literally. He loved babies and toddlers because they were not that much bigger or taller than him. So with the landlord, Sam's permission, Star was placed on a bar stool, where he happily stayed because now, in his mind, he was part of the conversation and the crowd, and not on the floor amongst legs.

One afternoon Barrie was standing at the bar doing what he was best at – talking, when he heard some gasps and saw the locals getting into a bit of a panic, calling Barrie over.

"The ducks gone mad!" they cried. Star was running up and down, around in circles and then back to the water bowl. Barrie calmly came over and laughed

"He is just a little boy having a mad five minutes. He does it all the time." With that, everyone relaxed and just enjoyed watching him while he dipped his beak back into the water and then would almost fling himself away, run very quickly in a big circle and then back to the water bowl again. We have no idea why he does it, but as Barrie said, we have to remember he is just like a little boy, really. It is no different to when he is getting his beak inquisitively into everything, nudging keys off the side, and generally being like a little toddler.

He did the same each time I counted up the money from their day out. I learned very quickly that I had to build a barrier around me as Star liked nothing more than to put his beak in, usually pulling out a coin or two. Each and every time he pulled some money out I would panic that he would swallow it. And each and every time Barrie would tell me I was overreacting as, after all, he saw Star taking money out of people's hands all the time and putting it in the bucket. I guess it was Star's way of making sure we were under no illusion that the majority of the money raised was on the back of Star being Star and not just because it was for charity.

Barrie and Star truly had their double act down to a fine art now. As much as the people enjoyed meeting Barrie and Star, and actually making their day, Barrie also had fun. It brought out his wicked sense of humour. During the holiday season, an extended family came over to see Star. At least three generations were within this group. It turned out they were from *up North*. Being a Manchester lad himself, Barrie realised he could have some real fun here. He told them, as he often did to those who he felt would really enter into it, that Star enjoyed several pints after a hard day's work.

"Only a couple of pints?" the young man said.

"After a hard day's work he would surely need more than that? What about cigarettes? Does he smoke?"

"Oh yes. Unfortunately he is a pack-a-day smoker, especially when he and I are out on the pull on a Friday or Saturday night. He really goes for it then." Everyone was laughing until this lady came up, deadly serious, and spat in Barrie's face,

"How could you let him drink and smoke so heavily? I am reporting you to the RSPCA." And with that, she stormed off. We later found out that she did indeed put a call into them. They thought it was a crank caller.

On the note of drinking, on another occasion someone asked,

"How do you know when he is drunk?"

"I don't know," Barrie replied. "But I'll tell you this: he certainly has drinker's feet. A tip for you when you are out on the lash: wear flippers."

"Having said that," he went on to add, "don't ever try walking backwards in them!"

So how does Barrie get talking to people about Star drinking in the pub? Well, he begins with explaining that Star loves what he does, doesn't do it for a wage, and just expects his pint of real ale after a hard day's work. From there it becomes all ad lib and changes each and every time, depending on those he is talking to. But it usually goes a bit like this:

"Naturally I have to go into the pub with him as he is under age after all. It would be rude of me not to have a pint with him. I'm not selfish, you see. I put Star first. I would far rather be out shopping with the misses, or hoovering and dusting or something."

"Yeah right" is the usual retort. Or,

"Of course you do. How very good of you."

Sometimes he would get really lucky and the banter would go even further. Like one time when this young couple with two small children in tow, really did join in with the fun. They had already had the banter about Star going to the pub. The young dad then responded,

"You are a legend mate. A real legend." To which Barrie replied,

"You know people have called me a saint before now? And that is a hard thing to live up to."

"I know what you mean. Us saints have a hard time." At this his partner's eyes rolled upwards as if to say,

"Yeah right!"

"Oh you're one, too. There are not many of us around you know. We need to stick together. A real brotherhood. What's your name by the way?"

"Colin."

"Saint Colin. Yes, sorry I didn't recognise you, but I've heard about you. I'm Saint Barrie."

"Nope," replied the young man with a twinkle in his eye. "Never heard of you!"

One time when Barrie and Star were in the pub they often frequented, as was often the case being early afternoon, it was virtually empty with only one other guy there, who was sitting on a stool being propped up by the bar. Despite the early hour, he had obviously been there since opening time and was certainly on his way to an early bed! Barrie ordered his usual pint of real ale and started talking to the landlady. As usual, Star took his share of the pint. On hearing the voices, the guy looked up, noticing he was no longer alone. Then he looked down. His eyes widened as he looked at Star, then to the landlady, then into his pint: which was half full. With that the landlady said,

"It's all right, Malcolm. You're not hallucinating. There is a duck wearing a bow tie, drinking ale."

The guy looked so relieved. He took another look at the duck, downed the rest of his drink and said, "Thank **** for that! You can pull me another pint!"

Sometimes in the night I quite often have a chuckle to myself: Barrie talking in his sleep. Not just any old talking. You've guessed it - in Duck language. If that wasn't weird enough, now we were in the mobile home, therefore all on one level with Star's bedroom not far from ours, I would hear Star respond! Honestly. They could get a real conversation going between them that could go on for a while. The problem is though, I have never been very good at languages and therefore have never understood what they are saying to each other. I'm also not sure whether Star is awake or actually sleep talking back! I would like to say it's a fluke, but no. It happens pretty regularly. Odder still, I see a pair of eyes looking at me: it's Drake. Probably thinking the same as me and not really believing this himself. It has happened too many times to put it down to a dream of my own!

Now, you probably think that this is all a bit odd? Not to me. I call him Hayman and he quite often goes into a place I refer to as "Haymansland." I have known about this other world for years and he has always invited me in. However, I have always resisted the temptation as I suspect if I were to enter this world I would find a cross between

Neverland, Nania and Willy Wonka's Chocolate Factory, complete with Umpa Lumpers and Munchkins! Yes it sounds like fun, but I wonder if I wouldn't have to be dragged out by men in white coats? Or never to return! Although Barrie is highly intelligent, he does live in his head an awful lot and with Star now as his side-kick, I am in no doubt that Star enters Haymansland quite regularly with him and thoroughly enjoys it. All very odd I grant you, but could I get away with passing this off as eccentric?

We now had quite a large collection of bow ties. Many of them had been donated. Not long after Star started wearing them, they met a lovely young lass. She was so enchanted with Star that she raced off after spending quite a considerable time with him, and then found them again not long afterwards, armed with a selection of bow ties. She had gone to all the charity shops and had purchased all the bow ties she could find with her own pocket money. Barrie was absolutely choked by this. Star was really chuffed too, and although they are a bit worn out now, still wears some of them today.

I have never been big on sewing, but I had to learn quickly how to adapt them for Star. Each time they were going out, whether it be collecting or otherwise, Barrie would line up a selection of them. Star in his own way, would select which one he wanted to wear that day. One thing about bow ties though, is that they are not very good in the rain. They get so soggy so quickly. So despite Star picking out his particular bow tie each time, Barrie would have to make sure that he took several with him.

Quite often they would be in the rain when out and about. Barrie, with his trademark cowboy hat, didn't mind the rain too much as long as it wasn't windy with it, but Star, being a duck, absolutely loved the rain. The only problem with that though, is that he also loved the puddles. Whenever there was a puddle, Star would be in it, drinking it, or standing there washing and preening in it. Passers-by would stop to watch. For Barrie this was not part of the act, but try telling a duck to stay away from the water!

Chapter Twenty-Nine

My temporary job didn't stop after two weeks. I was actually there for two months. It would have been longer had I not been offered another job: a six-month contract which sounded far more challenging, interesting, and exciting.

But as things seemed to be looking up for me, for Barrie and Star it seemed they had a new enemy out to cause trouble for them: a Big Issue seller. Up until then Barrie had got on very well with them. However, this particular one, for some reason just took an instant dislike to Barrie and Star. He would shout out some really abusive and horrible things with plenty of foul language. It wasn't said quietly either. Each and every time they found themselves in the high street at the same time, Barrie tried to do anything he could to avoid this guy as it was not just offensive to him, he was aggressive with it, and didn't care who was in earshot of his foul mouth, including young families. It got to the point where Barrie stopped a policewoman and told her about it. Having checked the CCTV footage it could be seen that this guy had an aggressive stance, but it couldn't be heard what was being said. And when they actually asked him, they were told that Barrie had provoked him. There was nothing that could be done other than to continue to try to avoid him.

So now he found that it was not just the councils, other charities and buskers might have a problem with them, it was also a Big Issue seller too. It is incredible to think that one man and his duck could upset these people just for trying to do something good and bring some joy into people's lives at the same time.

One thing I did do was put together our own bucket signage. We were determined to continue to raise money and awareness for the Children's Hospice, but also wanted to get a clear message across that Barrie and Star were in fact buskers. They collected money, yes. But they didn't just stand there like lemons with a collection tin. They put on a double act. So I designed a cover that had our own Star logo (designed the year before) alongside the Children's Hospice logo. And just to ensure there was no doubt, I also put the word *buskers* on there.

Armed with his new bucket, hopefully the troubles would calm down a little bit.

A little while later Barrie and Star were invited along to a Children's Hospice collection day in Exeter. Barrie was thrilled to be part of this, and a change of scene to boot. The support from the local community had been overwhelming, but he was feeling that they needed to spread their wings a little further. The locals could only be expected to dig so deep into their pockets for so long. And besides, Star was keen to make some more new friends.

They started in the main shopping centre. However, Star is not very good in enclosed spaces. Not only would he feel a bit bewildered amongst a load of legs – and like Barrie, many people wore blue jeans so he could feel confused and lost as to where his dad was, but also as his ears are actually in his nose he would struggle to hear Barrie calling him.

So they headed out onto the main street.

Despite being summer, it was not a hot day. It was overcast, but thankfully not cold or raining. They set off and immediately were surrounded. Star was on top form: showing off; conversing with his dad; taking the money from people's hands to put in the bucket; and even at times shaking the bucket with his beak if he felt no one was putting any money in! They came around by the cathedral and there was a group of sightseers with a tour guide. Barrie spotted them so he made sure he gave them a wide berth so not to interrupt them. But Star had a different idea and walked right into the middle of the group. Before long the guide realised that he was actually talking to himself as all the tourists were taking photos of Star. They obviously thought this was far more interesting than the history of the magnificent cathedral. Apologetically, Barrie tried to coax Star away from the group, but the only thing that worked was the actual tour guide leading them away in a different direction. However, only half the group went with him with the rest choosing to stay with Star for a little longer.

Once Star was satisfied that he had successfully got the attention he craved, he was then happy to move along with Barrie. They came across a couple of cafés and restaurants with lots of people sitting outside. There is always an awkward moment at times like these, where they could quite easily be asked to move on due to health and safety reasons, but on this occasion when the staff spotted them, one by one they came out to say hello. At one point it was debatable whether any staff were actually left to serve the customers. Not that they seemed to mind too much as they were also enjoying the view from the windows. Another café owner struck a deal with them; if they hung around the area for a while she would serve them tea and coffee as they were attracting more people to the area so it was good for business. Win, win all round. Not that Star was bothered as he knew that his dad had water and worms in his backpack ready for when he got peckish.

A little while later they moved on and found themselves within the shops. At this point Star decided to walk into a well-known opticians. When Barrie realised that he had gone into the shop, he walked in to apologise only to be faced with both grins and confused faces. Those trying on new glasses were looking at the lenses in a different light. Had the glasses made them hallucinate? A duck, or goose, wearing a bow tie appearing out of nowhere? And considering where they were, maybe their adverts were a lie?

Yet again, the day had been a roaring success, both from a group fundraising perspective, and also for Star. They had a change of scene, made loads of new friends, and made more people smile.

It was a good job that Barrie and Star were starting to spread their wings. Up until a short while ago they had considered South Molton a safe bet in terms of facing no threat as they were based almost exclusively to inside the pannier market. They had almost religiously gone each and every week on market day Thursday, and sometimes on the Saturday too, alongside the stallholders, even through the winter. Although the pannier market was under cover, when it was cold you really felt it. And the wind would gust through. More than once, Star was literally raised off the ground by the wind as it swept through from one end to the other.

They had so many supporters there including the town council staff. There were many who were drawn to the market not just for their weekly country shop, but also to see their friends, Barrie and Star. I think it is safe to say that Barrie was now a toy boy and favourite to many and Star a pin up for young and old alike.

The tide seemed to have turned. Although other charities that occasionally collected there were only allowed on the street, as per the licence they would have been granted for that day, they started to come into the market, and more than once made a scene, asking for Barrie to leave. At this point you would have thought the town council would have backed Barrie and Star. After all, they had acknowledged them as celebrities by putting them into their local tourist brochure along with letting them park for free. But sadly it appeared not to be the case.

This was highlighted on one particular Thursday when Barrie was with Star at the pannier market as he had been pretty much every week through all weathers. He was approached by a lady he recognised as being connected with one of the other charities. He had seen her about before where she had shown her disapproval at their presence. This occasion was no different. She stated very clearly that he had no right to be there and told him to leave. As calmly as he could, Barrie told her that they did have a right to be there and was staying put. The stallholders within earshot piped up too, telling her in their own way to leave him alone.

She stormed out.

Not long later, Barrie and Star were approached by some officials of the town, who wasted no time in telling Barrie that he had to leave as he was upsetting the other charity. He was not prepared to argue the toss, so left the market. However, being the actor, he changed his clothes and hat, waited for a while, and then went back in, unseen, blending in with the crowds. He spotted the said charity worker now standing a lot further into the market with her little tin, set off to the side sandwiched between two stalls. No smiles, no interaction. So having ousted Barrie and Star from their regular patch, was she truly collecting any more money now that they had left?

Despite huge support from the stallholders and visitors, the local council were backing off with their support. Once again Barrie and Star were being side-lined. This was a bitter pill to swallow. And the sad part of all this? It was the visitors and stallholders who were to miss out. Barrie and Star felt they had been run out of town. They no longer made regular visits to the little market town.

They desperately needed to find new areas to visit where they would be welcome by all. One of their new towns was right up on the northern most coast of Devon – Lynmouth. A beautiful town right by the sea. It was total new ground for Star and Barrie. It was a lovely, hot summer's day. On the journey there, driving through the beautiful country lanes, which were only just wide enough for two cars to pass in each direction, Barrie joined the queue of traffic that had formed behind one of the 38-mile-an-hour club. Being the beginning of summer and the first hot day of the season the traffic was heavy. Living in an area where tourists flock, it was accepted that there would be lots of traffic, and with the lanes being full of twists and turns there was no room for overtaking. But Barrie was quite happy with the slow drive.

He used to be a professional driver so automatically drove in his mirrors on every journey. In the car behind he noticed a young couple. Just then, at a most inappropriate part of the road, they overtook him. However, due to the heavy traffic, there was something coming from the other direction and they had to swerve very quickly in front of him. Fortunately he had left a large gap. Not only was Barrie's heart in his mouth, he also noticed a sign swinging from their back window saying "little person on board," and could see a child's head on the back seat. Why would you put your child's life in danger just to move up one place? The young family didn't get any further forward for several more miles after that, but stayed very close to the bumper of the car in front. Unfortunately we have all seen this before and can only wonder why they do it.

Arriving at Lynmouth, Star was a little wary at first. Like most animals he is habitual. As the area was unfamiliar, he stayed very close to his dad. As was becoming the norm, they were soon surrounded by intrigued, excited, and surprised onlookers. It didn't take long for Star to settle into his unique performance with his dad by his side.

After a very successful time in the coastal town they were on the drive back home and something very strange happened. In complete contrast to the journey there, coming back there was very little traffic. This time he was bobbing along quite nicely. He came around a bend and was presented with a long, straight stretch of road before the next bend. Still no traffic either way in front or behind him. But then he saw a dark, large, late model vehicle coming around the bend from the opposite direction. And then drive on the wrong side of the road, on Barrie's side and continued at speed. Barrie had time to flash his lights and put his foot on the brake. But the car continued to head towards them and fast. By this time, Barrie had actually stopped the car... waiting for the impact. It appeared that this car was driving in a very straight line, not swerving, just dead in line with Barrie's car. Was this it? The end of Barrie and Star? He always felt that he and Star would go together to the next world and maybe this was the moment. Into the sunset towards Haymansland? As he was stationary, on impact there would be no doubt he would not walk away from this. The larger, newer car would go straight over the top of them. They didn't stand a chance.

But then, at the very last minute the car swerved, missing them by millimetres and continued to speed off on the correct side of the road.

Somehow Barrie managed to drive slowly into a lay-by very close by and just sat there, catching his breath, trying to understand what had just taken place. It all happened in slow motion, but very quickly, too. He certainly hadn't caught the registration plate or made note of who was driving and whether they were alone. He was not even sure whether he had been able to see anything through their windscreen at all.

When he arrived back to The Manor I couldn't understand why he had stayed sitting in the car before coming in. Especially in the heat. Eventually he came in looking white as a sheet. Instead of animatedly telling me all about their day, he told me about what had happened on the journey back. It was all so very strange. I asked him whether it was foreign plates on the car. Maybe a foreigner had briefly forgotten that we drive on the left here? No, he was sure that wasn't the case. And they weren't swerving across the road so it didn't sound like the driver was under the influence of anything. How very odd. And Barrie was clearly shaken very badly by the whole experience. He told me that he genuinely thought it was the end. In those few seconds, as the car was speeding head-on towards him, he had accepted his fate and was just waiting for the impact. Frightening. The one saving grace that I could see with this though: obviously his heart was in decent shape as it could easily have brought on a heart attack for him, me, or anyone else who experienced something as horrendous as that. The only logical conclusion to make from this weird experience, without venturing into any dark *what if* scenarios, was that Barrie and Star were in the wrong place at the wrong time and had been very fortunate that they came away only shaken and not harmed.

Chapter Thirty

Barrie could be guilty of being somewhat naïve, unaware of the laws surrounding charity collecting, with the need of applying for and being issued a daily licence. Where the mix up came as to whether he was a collector or a busker, we're not really sure. It could be argued that by carrying the bucket, emblazoned with the Children's Hospice logo, that this was the time he was truly a collector. However the difference is, as their confidence grew, their personalities came out more and more, and Barrie and Star started fully interacting with the public. In addition to this, now having the bucket meant that people could give money almost anonymously – there are some people who donate who don't necessarily want or expect to be acknowledged. This way, they could throw money into the bucket as they were passing with no fuss made, no matter how big or small the donation was. Even if he was engrossed through interacting with the public, as soon as Barrie heard the money drop into the bucket, he always tried to acknowledge this and say thank you. Even if it was to their back as they scurried away. Sometimes, when counting up, we would find people had actually put notes in: £5 and £10. We were so pleased and chuffed, but sometimes Barrie was also gutted because he wasn't aware of the large donation at the time it happened and therefore wouldn't have acknowledged the person.

We all know the high streets are dying as it is well documented in all the different media forms. Life needs to be brought back into them and surely entertainment is one of the best ways of doing this? In the same vein, may I be so bold as to suggest that some charities need to be more creative in the way they raise money? Even in this current problematic financial climate, it would seem that people are still willing to donate to a good cause. Having said that, it is my belief that society of today also likes to be entertained. Why is it that Comic Relief and Children in Need are so successful? Because they provide entertainment to encourage us to give. Yes, all charities are a worthy cause and why shouldn't we all give something to them? However, it is an unfortunate realisation of today's society – many people want, and in some cases expect something back.

Barrie and Star don't just stand there with a begging bucket. They carry a bucket, yes. Money is donated to charity, yes. But they also work very, very hard to interact and connect with the public, make them smile, provide entertainment just like the PR engines behind the giants of Children in Need and Comic Relief.

So, are Barrie and Star collectors and therefore regulated by the councils based on a one hundred year old Act? There might be a few parts of this law that could be translated in today's world, but there is no getting away from the fact: 1916 was completely different and bares very little resemblance to the society we know today.

Or are they merely buskers who choose to give money to charity?

We will let you decide.

Chapter Thirty-One

Like most animals, Star can moult. His feathers literally just fall out when they are ready. But if we see a feather sticking out, we can't pull it out otherwise it would hurt him, like plucking a clump of hair out of your head. One day whilst out and about one of the feathers came off. A large one at that. One of the old dears was with them at the time and watched it happen. She asked Barrie if she could keep it. Of course she could. It's not like we had any use for them. And besides, we had loads coming out at home all the time. Barrie wouldn't have thought anything more of this as it wasn't really a big deal. However, a week or so later, this same old dear saw Barrie, and all smiles, recounted how later that day she found out that she had won £100 on the lottery. She had never won anything in her life up until then, so now saw the feather as lucky. We didn't want to advertise the fact too much as everyone would want his feathers and before we knew it, we could have a bald duck on our hands. However, we did start saving the feathers as they dropped!

One of the questions nearly always asked is how long ducks can live. An innocent question you might think? But actually this haunts Barrie. He loves Star so much and as they are pretty much joined at the hip, he couldn't imagine life without him. Despite this, he would dutifully reply that some ducks can live as long as twelve years. Obviously being different, who knows how long Star will be with us. When we had Hayman's Farm some of the ducks and chickens just died for no apparent reason. Star has just turned two years old and hopefully has many more years to follow.

Another thing people are always curious about is why. Why is Star different? Well, apart from our belief that he is wired differently, I also believe that he gets a lot of his confidence from Barrie. In many ways Star IS Barrie, but in the form of a duck. It was obvious from the beginning that Barrie and Star were kindred spirits. Barrie didn't train Star. He just recognised he was different and acted upon it. Star loves performing as much as Barrie. As Star has matured and grown into an adult duck, believe me, having seen the diva duck come out in him regularly at home, he would not do anything he doesn't want to do. Barrie and Star are two peas in a pod. They complement each other completely.

Despite all the troubles, Barrie and Star continue to go out to raise awareness and do what they can for the Children's Hospice and at the same time enhance the lives of so many people who meet them.

As I sit here writing, the dogs are having a snooze and Barrie is sitting nearby. Star is also here standing beside Barrie, resting his beak on his dad's leg as he so often does, content and happy.

There is one thing that absolutely everyone is in agreement with and cannot deny: Star is very special. Not only that, Star has proved that he is not just Barrie's duck. He is without doubt the people's duck. Barrie and I feel very privileged to be his minders.

Thank you Star, for enhancing lives in so many ways. We love you.

Epilogue

I have made a point of not mentioning the charities or councils who have caused so much upset to Barrie and Star. This is for good reason. We have absolutely no wish to bring any of them into any disrepute. At the end of the day they are all very good causes and we have no gripe with the work they do.

So how does Barrie feel about Star? Well, let's ask him...

I knew from the moment I saw him he was different. All the other ducklings were as cute as, but I just knew he was waiting for me. I recognised the performer in him almost straight away. When he didn't settle with his siblings, it seemed obvious to put him in my breast pocket and take him out with me. He happily stayed there with his little head stuck out.

Up until that point, Drake was top dog. I loved nothing more than working him at every opportunity but as time went on, Star overtook that. I still feel guilty about that as each day passes, and try not to leave Drake out, taking him with us every time.

I never knew where it was all heading but Star and I just became closer and closer.

I believe everything happens for a reason. I was forced into retirement and Star was sent to me as a real companion. I would have him with me the whole time and in the bedroom with me at night if I could, but at the same time I realise he needs his space, and I guess I need mine too. Once he goes into the cage, the night seems so long without him. It sounds awful because I obviously love my wife to bits, but I miss my duck when he is not with me. I sometimes have nightmares, that he is not there anymore or I have mislaid him. I will get up in the middle of the night and if I can't hear him I make a little noise, but if he still makes no sound, I have to lift the blanket just to check he is okay, even though I don't really want to disturb him. I don't say anything to him but we are silently connecting with each other. Once morning arrives, I let him out of the cage and we are together again.

What I go through, Star seems to go through. If I'm stressed, he's stressed. We have the same temperament and similar characteristics too: headstrong, fussy, determined, same *don't mess with me* attitude!

At first I thought it was all about me but then realised Star was here for a greater reason. He has a huge heart, and has this sixth sense for those who need comfort, support or just something to smile about. We are dedicated to the Children's Hospice but we would also like to go further than that and for Star to be the children's duck. All children matter. Few people know my name, referring to me as *the duck man* but everyone knows Star's name, and that is how it should be.

I could say we are each other's best friend but it is not as simple as that. We are truly soul-mates. I sometimes wonder if we actually share the same soul as we have become as one in so many ways. Sue realises and accepts this and so do the dogs. God willing, I will pop my clogs and he will pop his webs at the same time, as that would be the greatest kindness to us both, as neither will survive without the other.

We are what we are, and do what we do.

I love my duck and would give my life for him.

About the Author:

Born and raised in Chatham, Kent, Sue then went to university in London where she completed a degree in Leisure Management, including a gap year spent working in the Canadian Rockies. After working in London for a few years, she went backpacking in New Zealand and Australia. It was during her time working in Melbourne she met her husband Barrie and they returned to the UK together. After a few years living in Kent, they eventually moved and settled in Devon where they have lived for over 10 years. Sue and Barrie don't have children together, choosing animals instead. They currently have 2 dogs, Drake and Meggie, and their famous duck, Star.

The writing of "Star: The Story of One Duck's Rise to Fame" was a real surprise to Sue, who up until that point, had never thought of becoming an author. However, the incredible events taking place with Barrie and Star gave plenty of content where a story was just asking to be told.

From the author:

I hope you found as much enjoyment reading Star: The Story of One Duck's Rise to Fame as I did writing it. If so, please consider leaving a review on Amazon.

If you would like to stay updated on the newest releases from me or other authors published by MKSP, then simply follow this link and sign up for their newsletter.

I love connecting with my readers and would enjoy hearing from you. Here are some quick links to follow to stay connected.

Meet Sue Hayman on Facebook:
https://www.facebook.com/sue.hayman.73

Star's Facebook page:
https://www.facebook.com/profile.php?id=100002792047162&fref=ts

Twitter: @suehayman3

Printed in Great Britain
by Amazon.co.uk, Ltd.,
Marston Gate.